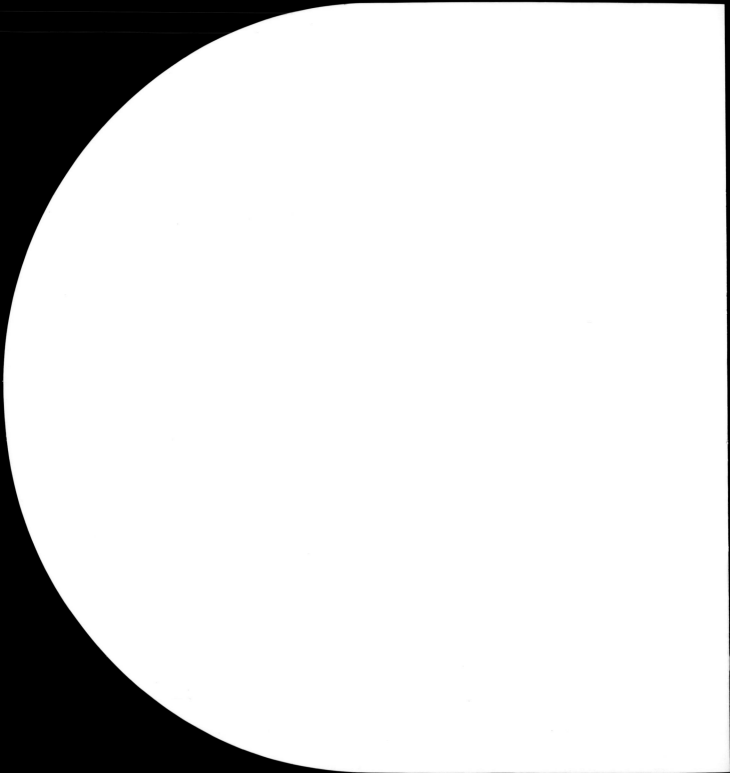

BASEBALL

TRIVIA

BASEBALL TRIVIA

LEW FREEDMAN

M
METRO BOOKS
NEW YORK

Designer: Danny Gillespie
Color Reproduction: Rival Colour

Metro Books
122 Fifth Avenue
New York, NY 10011

ISBN: 978-1-4351-2098-3

Printed and bound in China

1 3 5 7 9 10 8 6 4 2

Photo credits
Corbis: James L. Amos 77; Bettmann 13TR, 16, 19, 20, 23, 24, 25, 26, 27, 28, 32, 33, 41 BL & R, 42, 44, 45, 46, 47, 49, 51, 55, 57, 61, 62, 63, 66, 72, 78, 88, 91, 105, 107, 110T, 114, 115, 121, 122, 126, 132, 133, 134 (both), 135, 137 (both), 140L, 141, 146, 152, 153, 158; Walter G. Arce /Icon SMI 2-3; Dustin Bradford/Icon SMI 111; Mike Cassese/Reuters 15; Anthony J. Causi/Icon SMI 75; Henry Diltz 99; Peter Foley/epa 83; Joe Giza/Reuters 110B; Larry Goren/Icon SMI 29, 142B; C.J. Gunther/epa 69, 71; Lance Iversen/San Francisco Chronicle 118; Minnesota Historical Society 87; Guy Motil 109; John Munson/Star Ledger 143; Steve Nesius/Reuters 130; Neal Preston 85, 117; William Perlman/Star Ledger 98; Pool/Reuters 90; Reuters 34R, 95, 123, 142T, 144, 154; Wally McNamee 43; Robert Sorbo/Reuters 157; Michael Tureski/Icon SMI 56; Underwood & Underwood 17R, 35, 64 (inset), 84, 112, 147; Cliff Welch/Icon SMI 14.
Getty Images: 65 MLB Photos.
Istockphoto: Andrew Coleman 96; Laura Young 104.
The Kobal Collection: 36 Universal/Gordon.
Library of Congress: 6, 7 (all), 8 (both), 9T, 11, 12, 13 (L & BR), 17L, 21, 22 (both), 30, 31, 34L, 37, 40 (both), 50, 58 (both), 59, 61 (inset), 64, 76T, 79, 81, 86, 89, 92, 93, 96, 101, 106, 108, 113, 125, 129 (inset), 136 (all), 138 (both), 139 (both), 140R, 145, 148, 149, 150, 151, 156, 159.
Wikipedia: 76B, 119, 127, 128–129, 131; Keith Allison 9B, 39, 53, 70; Andrew Klein 41T.

Previous pages: A detail from Fenway Park.

Contents

Abner Doubleday was a Civil War general who was given credit by a Major League Baseball investigating commission report in 1907 as the inventor of the sport. While there is little evidence to support the claim, there is a Doubleday Field in Cooperstown, down the street from the Hall of Fame, and some still believe Doubleday's alleged connection to the origins of the game. Many scholars offer an alternate theory, giving Alexander Cartwright credit for adapting the English game of rounders and establishing many of the rules still in use today in the 1840s, though historians admit it is difficult to trace the invention of baseball to just one person.

"Honest John" Morrill, first baseman for the Boston Beaneaters, seen in 1887. In 1883 he took over as manager midseason and led the Beaneaters to the National League pennant.

Joe Birmingham was an outfielder with the Cleveland Naps, and is seen in 1911, the year before he became the Naps' manager.

What's in a Name?

- The **Chicago Cubs** were once the **Orphans**

- The **Boston Braves** were once the **Beaneaters**

- The **Cleveland Indians** were once the **Naps**

- The **Brooklyn Dodgers** were once the **Superbas** and also were once the **Bridegrooms**.

- A forerunner of the **Pittsburgh Pirates** was the **Allegheny Innocents**.

Edward B. Barger and William Bergen of the Brooklyn Superbas, in 1912. Catcher Bill Bergen was bought from the Reds in 1904 and is remembered as possibly the worst hitter in the majors: his career saw 3,028 at-bats and his batting average was .170. He was worth his place, however, for his defensive catching.

Right: Harry Wright.

Far right: 1869 Cincinnati Red Stockings.

8

HARRY WRIGHT, Man'g. Philas
GOODWIN & CO. New York.

Henry Chadwick invented the box score and worked diligently as a journalist and statistician to promote the modern rules of baseball. On his headstone in a Brooklyn cemetery is emblazoned the phrase, "Father of Base Ball."

FIRST NINE OF THE
CINCINNATI
(RED STOCKINGS) BASE BALL CLUB.

The first professional baseball team—where all players were paid—was the 1869 Cincinnati Red Stockings, managed by Harry Wright. Wright, born in England, was weaned on cricket, but adapted to baseball after moving to Ohio. He was the highest paid player on the team that year, making $1,200 for his dual role as field boss and center fielder.

Left: Harry Wright.

Below: Fernando Rodney.

Baseball teams first attempted to use uniform numbers to identify their players in the 1880s, but after brief experimentation the move fizzled. In 1929, the Cleveland Indians, then the New York Yankees, reintroduced player numbers on the backs of uniforms and by 1932 all 16 Major League clubs employed the device.

In 1893 the distance from the pitcher's mound to home plate was 55 feet, 6 inches. A committee of team owners made the decision to push the mound back in order to help hitters. It has been said that when the final plans were unveiled the handwriting of the note-taker was mistaken for 60 feet, 6 inches, rather than 60 feet, but others say that is mythology. However, 60-6 has been the hurling distance ever since. The pitching rubber, which anchored a thrower to one spot on the mound, was introduced at the same time.

"Take Me Out to the Ball Game"

Baseball's anthem, "Take Me Out to the Ball Game," was written by Jack Norworth in 1908 while riding a New York subway. The music was penned by Albert Von Tilzer. Neither man saw a baseball game until decades after the song became a hit. Norworth changed some of the verses in a rewrite in 1927, but the main chorus, known so well to fans who sing it during the seventh-inning stretch at games, remained the same.

Take me out to the ball game,
Take me out with the crowd.
Buy me some peanuts and Cracker Jack,
I don't care if I never get back,
Let me root, root, root for the home team,
If they don't win it's a shame.
For it's one, two, three strikes, you're out
At the old ball game.

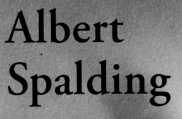

Albert Spalding

During the winter of 1913–1914, sporting goods impresario Albert Spalding organized a world tour showing off American baseball in such places as Ceylon, Egypt, and England, but other than a curiosity the tour made little impact in spreading the gospel of baseball. It was then quickly overshadowed by the start of World War I.

Right: Albert Spalding.

What's in a Name? Part II

In baseball's earlier days, players were routinely given nicknames. Match these Hall of Famers with their nicknames *(answers on page 14).*

CRAWFORD, DETROIT

Above: Sam Crawford.

1. Walter Johnson

2. Casey Stengel

3. Pepper Martin

4. Luke Appling

5. Mordecai Brown

6. Orlando Cepeda

7. Sam Crawford

8. Charles Comiskey

9. Frankie Frisch

10. Carl Hubbell

11. Rogers Hornsby

12. John McGraw

13. Branch Rickey

14. Paul Waner

15. Lloyd Waner

A. The Wild Horse of the Osage

B. Three-Finger

C. Wahoo

D. The Rajah

E. Big Poison

F. Little Poison

G. Cha Cha

H. The Old Perfessor

I. Meal Ticket

J. Little Napoleon

K. The Fordham Flash

L. Big Train

M. The Old Roman

N. The Mahatma

O. Old Aches and Pains

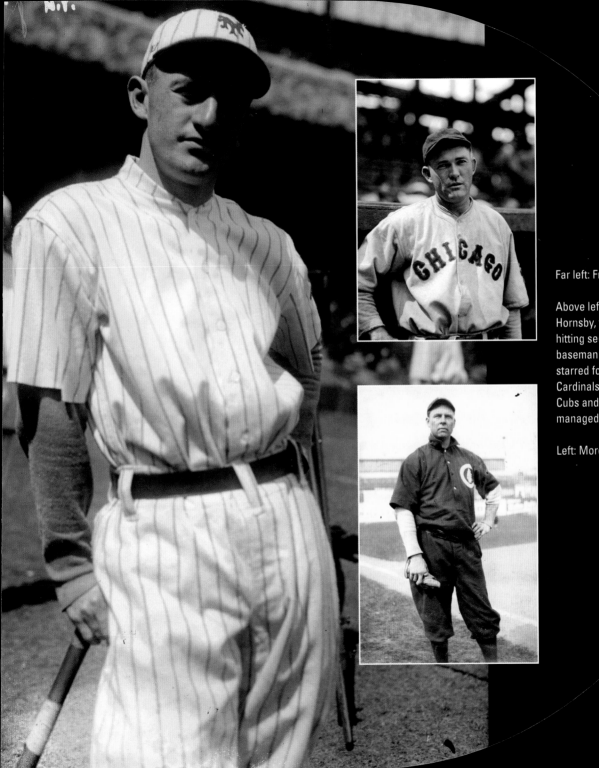

Far left: Frankie Frisch.

Above left: Rogers Hornsby, the greatest hitting second baseman of all-time, starred for the St. Louis Cardinals and Chicago Cubs and also managed the Cubs.

Left: Mordecai Brown.

Below: Tampa Bay Ray's outfielder Carl Crawford steals a base against the Boston Red Sox during a 2009 game at Tropicana Field. Crawford tied a record by swiping six bases in one game.

14

Nicknames of non-Hall of Fame players

Harry "Suitcase" Simpson
Lance Berkman, "Fat Elvis"
Adam Dunn, "Big Donkey"
Julio Franco, "Father Time"
Orlando Hernandez, "El Duque"
Carl Crawford, "The Perfect Storm"
Hideki Matsui, "Godzilla"
Joe Nathan, "Nathan's Famous"
David Ortiz, "Big Papi"
Frank Thomas, "The Big Hurt"
Darrell Evans, "Howdy Doody"
Al Hrabosky, "The Mad Hungarian"
Dennis Martinez, "El Presidente"
Bill "Spaceman" Lee
Don Zimmer, "Popeye"
Bill "Moose" Skowron

Left: Toronto Blue Jays' Frank Thomas.

Among the starting pitchers for the 1934 World Champion St. Louis Cardinals were hurlers named Dizzy, Daffy, and Dazzy—Dizzy Dean, his brother Daffy, and Dazzy Vance. Dizzy Dean and Dazzy Vance were elected to the Hall of Fame.

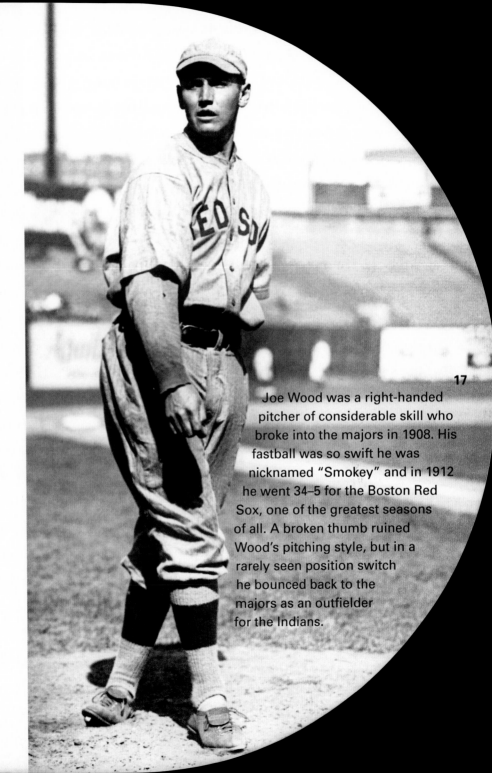

Slugger George Herman Ruth was best known as Babe Ruth. But he had several other nicknames, including "The Bam," "Bambino," "The Sultan of Swat," "The Colossus of Crash," "The King of Swing," and "The Terrible Titan."

Above: A young, lean Babe Ruth.

Left: St. Louis Cardinals brothers on the pitching mound. Dizzy (Jerome) Dean (R) and his younger brother Paul.

Right: Joe Wood.

Joe Wood was a right-handed pitcher of considerable skill who broke into the majors in 1908. His fastball was so swift he was nicknamed "Smokey" and in 1912 he went 34–5 for the Boston Red Sox, one of the greatest seasons of all. A broken thumb ruined Wood's pitching style, but in a rarely seen position switch he bounced back to the majors as an outfielder for the Indians.

Eccentric Owners

Hall of Famer Bill Veeck, who operated the Cleveland Indians, the St. Louis Browns, and the Chicago White Sox twice, is regarded as the most fan-friendly owner in history. He was responsible for installing the ivy in Wrigley Field when he was a young man, emphasized ladies' days, and installed the exploding scoreboard at Comiskey Park.

When he was trying to boost attendance as owner of the hapless St. Louis Browns in August of 1951, Bill Veeck famously sent a dwarf named Eddie Gaedel to the plate for an at-bat. Veeck snuck the 3'7" Gaedel onto the official roster through some late-night paperwork, outfitted him with a uniform displaying the number 1/8th on the back, and ordered him not to swing at a pitch. Naturally, Gaedel walked on four pitches. The Browns pinch-ran for Gaedel and Gaedel retains the distinction of being the shortest man ever to bat in the majors.

In the 1970s, during his second round of ownership of the Chicago White Sox, Bill Veeck introduced the idea of players wearing Bermuda shorts as part of their uniforms in order to stay cooler on the hottest days of the summer. He even had former players model the short pants outfit, but the suggestion was greeted with hostility by the current players and swiftly fizzled out.

19

Above: Creative baseball promoter and St. Louis Browns

20

One of the most eccentric owners of all was Charles O. Finley, the Chicago millionaire who took over the Kansas City Athletics, moved them to Oakland, and led them to several world championships. Finley promoted the use of orange-colored baseballs, argued for the creation of the designated hitter, and employed a live mule as a team mascot. He dressed his team in very bright green and gold uniforms and paid players $300 each to grow old-fashioned mustaches. He also second-guessed managers, argued with the commissioner's office over trades, and alienated players with outrageous comments.

Awards

The winningest pitcher in Major League history is Cy Young, who won 511 games in a career that ended in 1911 after 22 seasons.

In 1955, the year after Cy Young died, Major League Baseball instituted a new award. Presented to the best pitcher in the majors, the Cy Young Award was first given to Brooklyn Dodger Don Newcombe. Only one award was presented until 1966, but since 1967 a Cy Young winner has been designated for each league.

Far left: Charlie Finley.

Left: Cy Young.

In 1911, Major League Baseball decided to choose Most Valuable Player winners for each league for the first time. The honor was called the Chalmers Award and continued until 1931 when the Baseball Writers' Association of America took over the selection of MVPs. Ty Cobb of the Detroit Tigers won the first Chalmers Award in the American League and Frank Schulte of the Chicago Cubs won in the National League.

Above: Ty Cobb.

Above: Frank Schulte.

No Rookie of the Year Award was presented in Major League Baseball until 1947, and then only one was given out for both leagues. The first winner was Jackie Robinson of the Brooklyn Dodgers. The next year Alvin Dark of the Boston Braves took the honors, and starting in 1949 the award was given to the top newcomer in each league.

Jackie Robinson (1919–1972), a Brooklyn Dodger from 1947–1956, the first black major league baseball player of the 20th century. He was entered into the Baseball Hall of Fame in 1962.

The Negro Leagues

Top Negro League teams between the 1920s and 1950: the Kansas City Monarchs, owned by J. L. Wilkinson; the Homestead Grays, owned by Cumberland Posey; the Newark Eagles, owned by Effa and Abe Manley; and the Pittsburgh Crawfords, owned by Gus Greenlee.

Cool Papa Bell was said to be the fastest man in baseball history. He never played in the majors because of his skin color. Satchel Paige often told a story about Bell being so fast he could turn off the light switch and be under the covers in bed before the room went dark. Bell later revealed that when he and Paige shared a room there was a faulty light switch with a delay, making the tale true.

Powerfully built catcher Josh Gibson died of a brain tumor at age 35 in 1947 and never played a minute in the majors, but followers of black baseball say he might have been the slugging equal of Babe Ruth. Records are sketchy, but it has been suggested that in Negro Leagues and winter league play Gibson may have hit 800 home runs.

Right: Portrait of baseball great Josh Gibson in a Homestead Grays baseball uniform. Known as the "Black Babe Ruth" for his home run prowess, Gibson played for the Pittsburgh Crawfords and the Homestead Grays in the Negro Leagues. He never had the opportunity to play in the Major Leagues because he died a few months before Jackie Robinson's historic debut with the Brooklyn Dodgers.

The only woman in the National Baseball Hall of Fame is Effa Manley. Manley was co-owner of the Negro Leagues stalwart team the Newark Eagles from 1936 to 1948 and ran the club's business operations.

Major League players in the Hall of Fame who also played in the Negro Leagues: Hank Aaron, Willie Mays, Satchel Paige, Monte Irvin, Roy Campanella, Jackie Robinson, Ernie Banks, Larry Doby, and Willard Brown.

Above: Ernie Banks, Chicago Cubs infielder.

Integrating the Majors

Above: Chico Carrasquel.

Before a so-called "gentlemen's agreement" among owners took hold banning blacks, and prior to the breakthrough of Jackie Robinson in 1947, the first African-American player in the majors was Moses Fleetwood Walker. Walker played for Toledo in 1884.

There are dozens of Latin-American stars in the majors now, but the first genuine Latino Major League star was Cuban Adolfo Luque, who broke in with the Cincinnati Reds in 1914 and won 194 games in a 20-year career as a pitcher.

Miguel, or Mike, Gonzalez, was a Cuban-born catcher who in 1938 became the majors' first Hispanic manager when he filled in as field boss for the St. Louis Cardinals for the season's final 16 games. His record was 8–8.

The first black pitcher in the majors after Jackie Robinson broke the color line was Brooklyn's Dan Bankhead. Bankhead appeared in four games in 1947 and was out of the majors by 1951.

The first Latino All-Star was Chico Carrasquel. The Venezuelan shortstop represented the Chicago White Sox on the 1951 American League team, the first of four All-Star selections. Carrasquel's popularity in his home country helped create ambition for future Venezuelan shortstop stars Luis Aparicio, Davey Concepcion, Omar Vizquel, and Ozzie Guillen.

Right: Manager Bill Jurges (R) of the Boston Red Sox, and Pumpsie Green, who became the first African American ever to play for the Red Sox.

The Boston Red Sox were the last Major League team to integrate its roster after Jackie Robinson broke the color barrier with the Brooklyn Dodgers in 1947. It was not until 1959 that the Red Sox integrated by retaining infielder Pumpsie Green for the big-league roster.

The first African-American coach in Major League Baseball was Buck O'Neil. The former Negro Leagues star and manager of the Kansas City Monarchs began scouting for the Chicago Cubs in the 1950s and became a coach in 1962.

Emmett Ashford became the first African-American Major League umpire on April 11, 1966.

Minnie Minoso is a unique character in baseball annals. A dark-skinned Cuban, Minoso was the first black player for the Chicago White Sox and was a seven-time American League All-Star. However, long after his retirement from regular play, promotional wiz owner Bill Veeck, and later his son Mike Veeck, brought Minoso back to professional ball for cameo hitting appearances. These brief returns made Minoso baseball's only seven-decade player and he wears a

In a 1971 game, the Pittsburgh Pirates become the first team to field an all-black lineup. The lineup: pitcher Dock Ellis, catcher Manny Sanguillen, first baseman Al Oliver, second baseman Rennie Stennett, shortstop Jackie Hernandez, third baseman Dave Cash, left fielder Gene Clines, center fielder Roberto Clemente, and right fielder Willie Stargell. Lauded as a pioneer, Manager Danny Murtaugh said he never even noticed he had put nine men of color on the field simultaneously.

Hall of Fame outfielder Frank Robinson became the first black manager when chosen to lead the Cleveland Indians in 1975. The second black manager was Larry Doby, who took over the White Sox briefly in 1978. Doby was also the second modern era black player, following Jackie Robinson, in 1947, and the first black player in the American League.

Above: Pioneering manager Frank Robinson last managed the Washington Nationals.

The Fall Classic

The first official World Series pitting pennant winners from the National League and the American League was held in 1903. The Pittsburgh Pirates represented the NL and the Boston Red Sox (then called simply the Americans) represented the AL. Boston won, five games to three in the best-of-nine format. Among the stars participating were Cy Young, pitching for Boston, and Honus Wagner, playing shortstop for Pittsburgh.

Since the modern World Series began in 1903, there have been two seasons when no champion was crowned. In 1904, New York Giants manager John McGraw refused to play the winners of the upstart American League. In 1994, baseball players were on strike and the last portion of the regular season, the playoffs, and World Series were cancelled.

Right: John McGrew.

Far Right: The Cubs play the Giants in 1908. The Cubs would go on to win the World Series—their last victory.

GIANTS

OF THE
NEW YORK NATIONALS

The last time the Chicago Cubs and the Chicago White Sox met in the World Series was 1906. The Cubs won 116 regular-season games that year to the White Sox' 93, but the White Sox upset the favored North Side team.

The Chicago Cubs last won the World Series in 1908, more than a century ago and counting. The last time the Cubs reached a World Series was 1945.

Fans of the Chicago Cubs sometimes blame "The Billy Goat Curse," for keeping their favorite team out of the World Series since 1945 and preventing the team from winning a World Series since 1908. In 1945, Bill Sianis, owner of the Billy Goat Tavern, a Chicago landmark, brought his pet goat to Wrigley Field, but was denied admission to a World Series game against the Detroit Tigers. When he was turned away and was insulted by being told that his goat smelled, Sianis supposedly placed a curse on the franchise, saying the Cubs would never again win the Series. Despite many attempts at exorcising it—including participation from Sianis' descendants—the Cubs have not come close to winning a World Series since.

The 1989 World Series was supposed to be special because it pitted the San Francisco Giants against the Oakland Athletics, the two Major League teams in the San Francisco Bay area. However, it proved to be more exciting than bargained for because of the Loma Prieta earthquake that struck before the third game of the Series, shaking Candlestick Park with thousands of fans present. Although it was a four-game sweep for Oakland, the Series took from October 14 to October 28 to complete because of damage done by the quake that among other things wrecked the Bay Bridge. The Series was put on hiatus for 10 days in respect for the 63 killed by the magnitude 7.1 shake. Since the earthquake struck as the time for the first pitch for Game 3 approached, it became the first quake to be broadcast on live television.

Below: San Francisco, California: Candlestick Park after an earthquake cancelled game 3 of the 1989 World Series.

Home runs hit to end a World Series: in 1960 Bill Mazeroski won the seventh game and the title for his Pittsburgh Pirates with a home run in the bottom of the ninth inning; in 1993 Joe Carter won the sixth game and the title for his Toronto Blue Jays with a home run in the bottom of the ninth.

33

Above: Pirate Bill Mazeroski is greeted by fans and fellow players after his ninth inning homer in the 1960 World Series.

After terrorists attacked the World Trade Center in New York, the Pentagon in Washington, D.C., and other aircraft on September 11, 2001, the Major League baseball season halted. Baseball was shelved until September 17, and with the Yankees in the playoffs and World Series, extra emotion was involved when play resumed and continued into October. Memorable renditions of "God Bless America" were sung during the seventh-inning stretch at Yankee Stadium. There was a suggestion that more people than usual around the country were rooting for the New Yorkers to win the World Series, but the Yankees lost a seven-game series to the Arizona Diamondbacks.

Right: Harry Hooper.

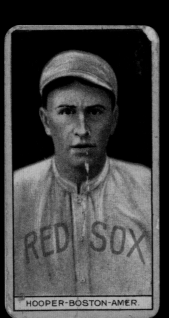

Above: Jessica Simpson smiles after singing "God Bless America" during the seventh inning stretch of Game 6 of the 2001 World Series.

When the Boston Red Sox won the World Series in 2004, it had been 86 years since their last title. In 1918, their stars included pitcher Babe Ruth (before his trade to the Yankees) and outfielder Harry Hooper. In 2004 their stars included pitcher Pedro Martinez and slugger David Ortiz.

HOOPER-BOSTON-AMER.

When the Chicago White Sox won the World Series in 2005, it had been 88 years since their last title. In 1917, their stars included pitcher Red Faber and supreme hitter Shoeless Joe Jackson. In 2005, their stars included pitcher Mark Buehrle and slugger Paul Konerko.

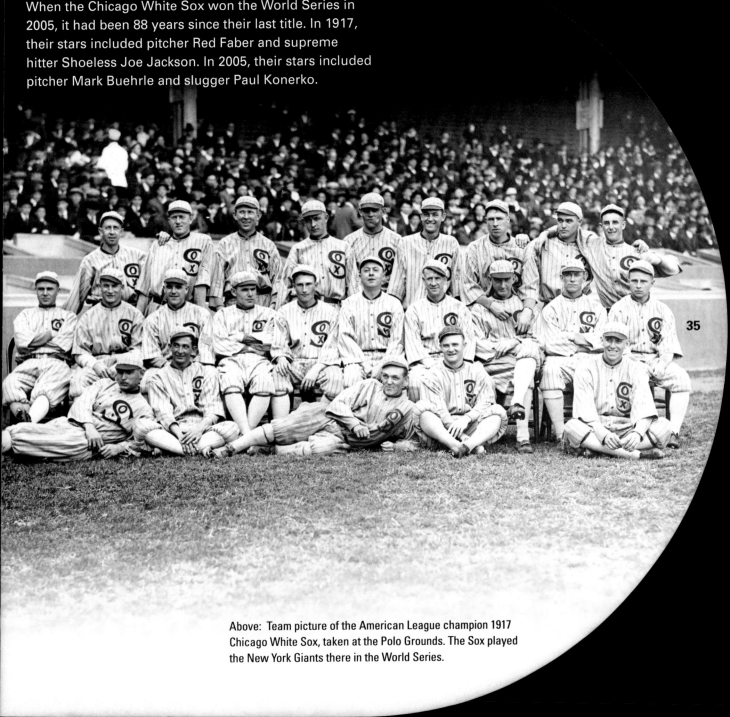

35

Above: Team picture of the American League champion 1917 Chicago White Sox, taken at the Polo Grounds. The Sox played the New York Giants there in the World Series.

Baseball on the Silver Screen

Classic baseball movies include: *The Natural*, starring Robert Redford and Glenn Close; *Bull Durham* and *Field of Dreams*, both starring Kevin Costner; *A League of Their Own*, starring Tom Hanks and Geena Davis; *Major League*, starring Tom Berenger and Charlie Sheen; *Bang the Drum Slowly*, starring Robert De Niro and Michael Moriarty; *The Bingo Long Traveling All-Stars*, starring Billy Dee Williams; and *Eight Men Out*, starring John Cusack, John Mahoney, and Charlie Sheen.

Below: Ray Liotta and Kevin Costner in *Field of Dreams*. Ray Liotta played "Shoeless Joe" Jackson who was banned from playing after the infamous Black Sox World Series fixing incident.

Baseball Literature

Notable baseball books include: *Shoeless Joe* by W. P. Kinsella, *The Pitch That Killed* by Mike Sowell, *Maybe I'll Pitch Forever*, by Satchel Paige and David Lipman, *Veeck— As In Wreck* by Bill Veeck and Ed Linn, *Babe: The Legend Comes to Life*, by Robert Creamer, *Joe DiMaggio: The Hero's Life*, by Richard Ben Cramer, *Sandy Koufax: A Lefty's Legacy*, by Jane Leavey, and *Luckiest Man: The Life and Death of Lou Gehrig*, by Jonathan Eig.

Above: The film *Field of Dreams* was taken from W.P. Kinsella's book *Shoeless Joe*. Here's the real "Sholess Joe" Jackson in a Cleveland Indians uniform.

Wizards with the Wood

Rogers Hornsby's .424 batting average in 1924 is the highest average of the modern era (since 1900). However, the Hall of Fame second baseman's best year was eclipsed by the all-time mark of .440 recorded by Boston's Hugh Duffy in 1894.

Hall of Fame outfielder Al Kaline is the youngest player ever to win a batting title at 20 years old. Kaline, who broke into the majors at 18, won the American League crown with a .340 average in 1955.

One of the greatest batting feats a hitter can accomplish is winning the Triple Crown—leading his league in home runs, RBIs, and batting average. The achievement has been recorded only 14 times, the first by Tip O'Neill in 1887 and the last by Carl Yastrzemski in 1967. Rogers Hornsby and Ted Williams are the only players to do it twice.

Minnesota Twins star
Mauer became the firs
catcher to lead the
American League in
batting when he hit .3
in 2006. He won a sec
batting title in 2008 ar
third in 2009.

Left: Joe Mauer.

Two players have stroked seven hits in a single, nine-inning game, one before the modern era and one since. Wilbert Robinson collected seven safeties for the Baltimore Orioles in 1892 and Rennie Stennett did likewise for the Pittsburgh Pirates in 1975.

Left: Later picture of "Uncle Robbie" Robinson when manager of the Brooklyn Robins, 1916. He was inducted into the Baseball Hall of Fame in 1945. He played 1,316 games as a catcher and while manager of Brooklyn the team was nicknamed the Robins in his honor.

OUR BASEBALL HEROES.

CAPTAINS OF THE TWELVE CLUBS IN THE NATIONAL LEAGUE.

Ichiro Suzuki of the Seattle Mariners holds the record for the most hits in a single season. His 262 base hits in 2004 broke George Sisler's old record of 257 set in 1920.

Left: Ichiro Suzuki.

Below: New York Yankees' star centerfielder Mickey Mantle was one of the best switch-hitters of all-time. His ambitextrous skill allowed him to bat from both the right- and left-hand sides of the plate. That ability foiled opposing managers' pitching strategy innumerable times. Mantle was the first switch-hitter to swat home runs from both sides of the plate in American League history.

Switch hitters are a baseball rarity. Few can hit equally as well from either side of the plate. Some of baseball's best switch hitters: Mickey Mantle, Pete Rose, Martin Dihigo, Eddie Murray, Frankie Frisch, Chipper Jones, Tim Raines, Chili Davis, Reggie Smith, Willie Wilson, George Davis, Carlos Beltran, Roberto Alomar, Lance Berkman, and Bernie Williams.

Home Run Heroes

Babe Ruth was famous for hitting 60 home runs in 1927, but as he improved as a slugger, and as an indicator of his dominance, Ruth also set marks for being the first player to hit 30, 40, and 50 home runs in a season.

Babe Ruth's final home runs came when he was briefly employed by the Boston Braves in 1935. He smacked three home runs in one game on May 25 against the Pittsburgh Pirates. That gave him a record total of 714 for his career, a mark that stood for 39 years until Hank Aaron surpassed it in 1974.

Above: Hank Aaron at bat prior to hitting his 714th home run to tie Babe Ruth's record at Riverfront Stadium in Cincinnati, Ohio.

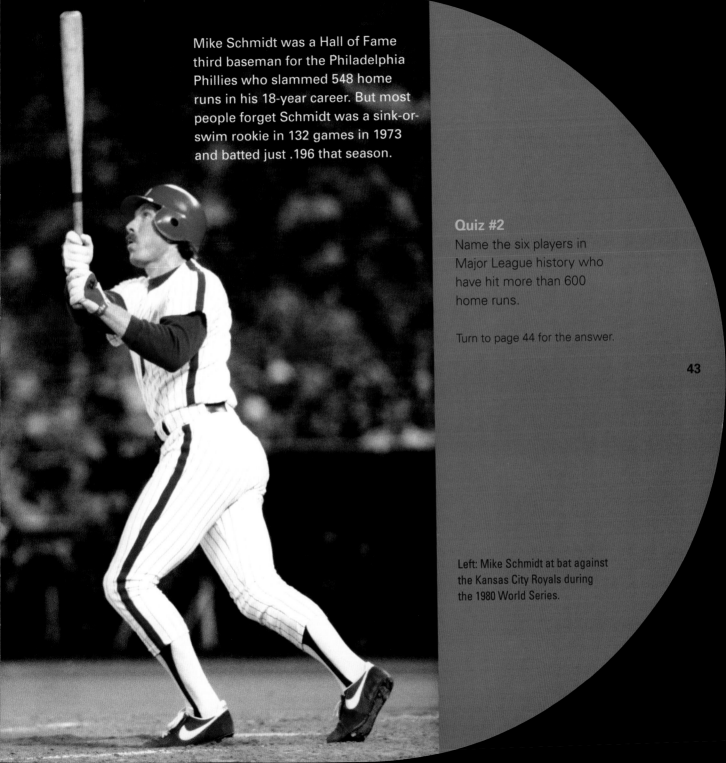

Mike Schmidt was a Hall of Fame third baseman for the Philadelphia Phillies who slammed 548 home runs in his 18-year career. But most people forget Schmidt was a sink-or-swim rookie in 132 games in 1973 and batted just .196 that season.

Quiz #2
Name the six players in Major League history who have hit more than 600 home runs.

Turn to page 44 for the answer.

Left: Mike Schmidt at bat against the Kansas City Royals during the 1980 World Series.

Masters of the Mound

Pitchers have struck out 20 players in a nine-inning game just four times in history. Roger Clemens did it twice, in 1986 and 1996. Kerry Wood and Randy Johnson also own a share of the record.

Dating back to the first in 1880, there have been 18 perfect games thrown in Major League history, where no runner has reached base against a pitcher. Of those, 17 occurred in the regular season and only one, tossed by New York Yankee Don Larsen, was in the World Series. Larsen's gem was recorded on October 8, 1956 in a 2–0 triumph over the Brooklyn Dodgers.

Left: Yogi Berra congratulates Don Larsen on his perfect game.

44

Answers to Quiz #2: Barry Bonds, 762; Hank Aaron, 755; Babe Ruth, 714; Willie Mays, 660; Ken Griffey Jr., 627 (still active); and Sammy Sosa, 609

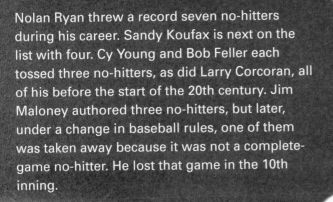

Nolan Ryan threw a record seven no-hitters during his career. Sandy Koufax is next on the list with four. Cy Young and Bob Feller each tossed three no-hitters, as did Larry Corcoran, all of his before the start of the 20th century. Jim Maloney authored three no-hitters, but later, under a change in baseball rules, one of them was taken away because it was not a complete-game no-hitter. He lost that game in the 10th inning.

Nolan Ryan's pitching career was notable for its longevity—a record 27 years between 1966 and 1993—and also for the phenomenal numbers he accumulated. Ryan won 324 games and lost 294 in 807 games, 773 of them starts. He pitched 5,386 innings and struck out a record 5,714 batters. He led his league in strikeouts 11 times, including six times striking out more than 300 men in a season. Ryan became president of the Texas Rangers ball club in 2008.

Left: Texas Rangers pitcher Nolan Ryan throws to the plate against the Mariners at the Kingdome.

Left: Bob Feller was considered a boy wonder when he joined the Cleveland Indians as a teenager in 1936. He quickly emerged as a star, but his prime years on the mound were interrupted by a 44-month stint in the Navy during World War II.

Hall of Fame pitcher Bob Feller was signed by the Cleveland Indians off his family farm in Van Meter, Iowa, for $1 and an autographed baseball. Feller was just 17 when he made his Major League debut in 1936 and went 5–3. Considered one of the fastest pitchers of all time, Feller won 266 games, but would likely have won many more if he had not lost three-plus seasons in his prime fighting in World War II.

Perhaps the greatest five-man starting pitching rotation for one year belonged to the Cleveland Indians of 1954. The Indians finished 111–43 and won the American League pennant that season behind the arms of Early Wynn (23 wins), Bob Lemon (23), Bob Feller (13), Mike Garcia (19), and Art Houtteman (15), but lost the World Series to the New York Giants in an upset. Wynn, Feller, and Lemon went on to the Hall of Fame.

With 373 career victories, righthander Grover Cleveland Alexander is one of the winningest pitchers of all time. Alexander spent 20 years in the National League playing for the Phillies, the Cubs, and the Cardinals. He won at least 30 games three times in a season and three other times won at least 27. Nicknamed "Old Pete," Alexander was portrayed in a movie about his life by then-actor and future president Ronald Reagan.

Satchel Paige's age was a great mystery throughout his career, though his date of birth was eventually firmed up as July 7, 1906. Paige sneered at age. After being prevented from playing in the majors in his prime because he was black, Paige made his Major League debut at age 42 in 1948 and was the first African American to pitch in the World Series. In 1965, at age 59, Paige threw three innings of one-hit ball for the Kansas City Athletics against the Red Sox.

Left: Grover Cleveland Alexander.

In 1968, Denny McLain won 31 games for the Detroit Tigers. It was the first time any pitcher had won as many as 30 since Dizzy Dean's 30–7 record in 1934, and it is the last time any pitcher has won 30 games in a season. McLain ultimately served prison time for drug trafficking and embezzlement, but has rebounded more than once to become a popular radio show host in Detroit and to write a blog for a Detroit sports magazine

The acknowledged best game ever pitched was thrown by the Pittsburgh Pirates southpaw Harvey Haddix in May of 1959. Haddix retired the first 36 Milwaukee Braves he faced in order, exceeding by three innings the normal perfect game. However, Haddix lost 1–0 in the 13th inning and years later Major League Baseball declared that it was not an official perfect game.

Quiz #3

Cy Young is the winningest pitcher of all time with 511 victories. Can you name the nine pitchers who fill out the top 10 in all-time victories? See the answer on page 50.

Below: Denny McLain pitching during first game of the World Series in 1968.

Answers to Quiz #3

2) Walter Johnson, 417;

3) (tie) Grover Cleveland Alexander and Christy Mathewson, 373;

5) Pud Galvin, 364;

6) Warren Spahn, 363;

7) Kid Nichols, 361;

8) Greg Maddux, 355;

9) Roger Clemens, 354;

10) Tim Keefe, 342.

Right: Walter Johnson.

Far right: Carl Hubbell.

JOHNSON, WASHINGTON

Hall of Fame pitcher Carl Hubbell, who spent his entire 16-year career with the New York Giants, was closely identified with one pitch—the screwball. A backwards curve that is delivered by turning the wrist inwardly instead of outwardly upon release, the screwball puts considerable stress on the arm.

Although the New York Yankees are the winningest team of all time, they have never had a star pitcher who came close to winning 300 games with the franchise. The club's all-time winner is Whitey Ford, who collected 236 victories.

51

Record-setting Relievers

● In 1959, Roy Face was the key relief pitcher for the Pittsburgh Pirates. His season record of 18–1 is the best ever for a reliever and his winning percentage of .947 is the best by any pitcher in Major League history.

● The pitcher who appeared in the most Major League games was reliever Jesse Orosco. In 24 seasons, Orosco, who was most closely identified with the New York Mets, appeared in 1,252 games.

● The pitcher who appeared in the most games during one regular season was Los Angeles Dodger reliever Mike Marshall. Marshall was called out of the bullpen 106 times in 1974. He won 15 games and recorded 21 saves. He also threw 208 1/3 innings, more than double what late-inning closers throw in today's game.

● The record for most saves in a single season was recorded by the Los Angeles Angels' Frankie Rodriguez in 2008. Rodriguez notched 62 saves, became a free agent, and signed with the New York Mets.

Right: Francisco Rodriguez.

53

What's in a Name? Part III

Hall of Famer Hank Aaron is the first player listed in the Baseball Encyclopedia's alphabetical order records under hitters. David Aardsma, who made his Major League debut in 2004 and in 2009 was a reliever for the Seattle Mariners, is the first one listed under pitchers.

Catcher Jarrod Saltalamacchia, who broke into the majors in 2007, has the longest name in Major League history and his last name barely fits on the back of his uniform in an arc.

Against the Odds

Pete Gray was a one-armed outfielder for the St. Louis Browns for one season during World War II, batting .218 in 77 games.

Monte Stratton was a solid starting pitcher for the Chicago White Sox in the late 1930s (he had played in one All-Star game), but he wounded himself in a hunting accident during the offseason after the 1938 campaign. Stratton fell and a pistol he was carrying fired into his right leg. Doctors had to amputate to save him. Stratton worked doggedly to come back, struggling to find his proper balance on an artificial leg. Stratton spent years playing in the minors or on semi-professional teams, but could not regain his full abilities to play again in the majors. However, he did win 18 games for a Class C team. The player's tale of determination was chronicled in a movie called *The Stratton Story*, in which Stratton was played by Jimmy Stewart.

Jim Abbott, when he was a
Los Angeles rookie pitcher.

Jim Abbott inspired a
generation of fans as a
starting pitcher for several
teams in the 1990s by
winning 87 games, including
a no-hitter, despite being
born without a right hand.
Abbott, a college star at
Michigan and an Olympian,
threw the ball left-handed,
and then swiftly shifted his
glove from under his arm to
his left hand.

Glove Men

The longest errorless streak in history by any player at any position is the 2,002 clean chances handled by Boston Red Sox first baseman Kevin Youkilis between July 4, 2006 and June 6, 2008. Most impressive is that first base is a position where the ball is handled frequently; it seems more likely the record would be held by an outfielder. However, the record for an outfielder is the 938 chances by Darren Lewis in the early 1990s. He even switched teams during the streak, going from the Oakland Athletics to the San Francisco Giants. The second longest position streak overall is at catcher, where the St. Louis Cardinals' Mike Matheny played error-free for 1,565 chances between August 2002 and August 2004.

Below: First baseman Kevin Youkilis #20 tries to pick off pinch runner Eric Patterson #1.

The Gold Glove Awards were created in 1957 to honor the top fielder in each league at every position. Several highly respected players have held virtual monopolies on the award at their main position over the years, including National League pitcher Greg Maddux, who won 18 times before retiring in 2008. Southpaw Jim Kaat won 16 Gold Gloves as a pitcher. Other players who have been dominant: catcher Ivan Rodriguez, 13 Gold Gloves; first baseman Keith Hernandez, 11 Gold Gloves; second baseman Roberto Alomar, 10 Gold Gloves; shortstop Ozzie Smith, 13 Gold Gloves; third baseman Brooks Robinson, 16 Gold Gloves, and outfielders Roberto Clemente and Willie Mays, 12 Gold Gloves each.

Ken Griffey Jr., Al Kaline, and Andruw Jones won 10 Gold Gloves each patrolling the outfield.

57

Left: Willie Mays in 1955.

Great Infields of Lore

The Philadelphia Athletics quartet that manned first, second, third, and shortstop between 1911 and 1915 was known as "The $100,000 Infield" for their spectacular value. Stuffy McInnis, Eddie Collins, Jack Barry, and Frank "Home Run" Baker never would have imagined how underpaid $100,000 would have made them 100 years later.

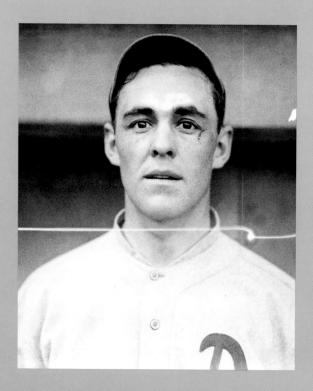

Above: Stuffy McInnis.

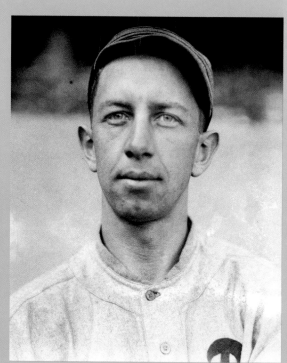

Above: Eddie Collins.

In the early part of the 20th century, the Chicago Cubs featured a double-play combination immortalized in poetry. Shortstop Joe Tinker, second baseman Johnny Evers, and first baseman Frank Chance were eventually all selected for the Hall of Fame. The unheralded third baseman in the group was Harry Steinfeldt. He didn't make the cut in the poetry or the Hall voting.

Above: Joe Tinker and Frank Chance.

These are the saddest of possible words:
   "Tinker to Evers to Chance."
Trio of bear cubs, and fleeter than birds
   Tinker and Evers and Chance.
Ruthlessly picking our gonfalon bubble,
   Making a Giant hit into a double—
Words that are heavy with nothing but trouble:
   "Tinker to Evers to Chance."

Speed Merchants

Stealing home is a lost art in baseball. The career record for the most times swiping home plate is owned by Ty Cobb, with 54, who retired in 1928. Second on the list is Max Carey, who stole home 33 times and retired in 1929.

The undisputed greatest leadoff hitter in baseball history is Rickey Henderson, elected to the Hall of Fame in 2009. Henderson is the game's all-time leader in runs scored with 2,295, and in stolen bases with 1,406. He stole a single-season record of 130 bases in 1982, one of three seasons he stole 100 or more bases. Henderson also collected a milestone 3,055 hits and has the second most walks in history with 2,190.

Growing up in difficult circumstances in Detroit, Ron LeFlore became entangled in a life of crime. He was serving a sentence for armed robbery at the state prison in Jackson, Michigan, when then-Tigers manager Billy Martin discovered his baseball abilities in 1973. Eventually, as a 26-year-old rookie, LeFlore made the Tigers roster as an outfielder and became an excellent hitter and stolen-base threat. He played nine years and more than 1,000 games in the majors, and a movie called *One In A Million* was made about his life.

Inset: Max Carey.

Right: Oakland A's Ricky Henderson ready to notch his 109th stolen base in 1982.

CAREY-PITTSBURG-NAT.

61

Field Leaders

The legendary Connie Mack, who managed his Philadelphia Athletics teams while wearing a suit instead of a baseball uniform, owns managing records due to his longevity. Mack managed the club for 53 years. He set the record for most managing victories with 3,731 and most managing defeats with 3,948. His teams won five World Series.

Above: Connie Mack.

Right: Cap Anson led the Chicago Cubs to five National League pennants in the 1880s.

ANSON, (1st Base, CHICAGO.

CHICAGO

OLD JUDGE & GYPSY QUEEN CIGARETTES

Billy Martin came to prominence as a New York Yankee second baseman in the 1950s. He had a successful managerial career turning around such franchises as the Detroit Tigers, Texas Rangers, Minnesota Twins, and the Yankees. Martin and Yankee owner George Steinbrenner were foils, however, and Martin was hired and fired to handle the Yankees a remarkable five times.

Major League managers who won the most pennants in their careers: Casey Stengel and John McGraw each won 10 pennants. Joe McCarthy won eight pennants.

Some famous player-managers, a role that has long disappeared from Major League ball: Lou Boudreau, Bucky Harris, Pete Rose, Frank Robinson, Ty Cobb, Joe Cronin, Cap Anson and Rogers Hornsby. There has not been a player-manager since Rose departed from the Cincinnati Reds' lineup in 1986.

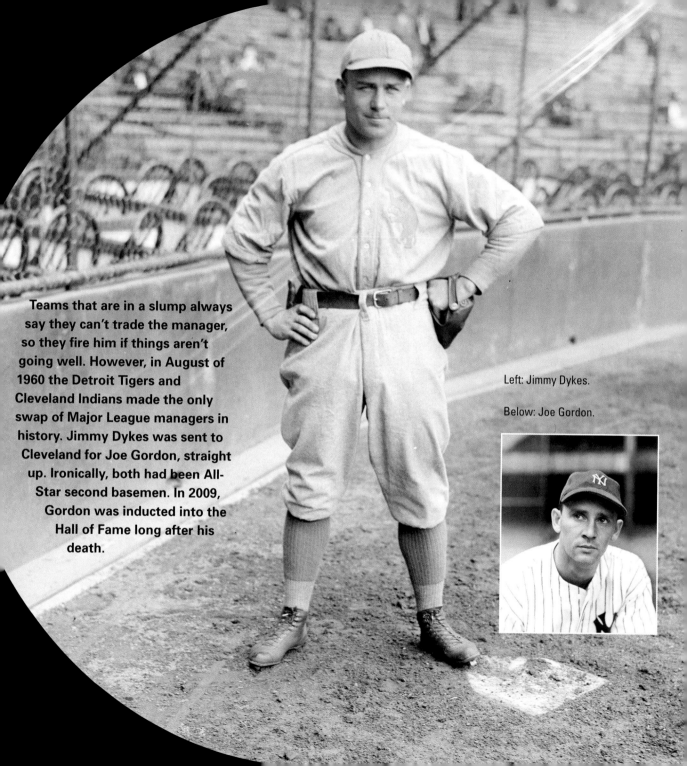

Teams that are in a slump always say they can't trade the manager, so they fire him if things aren't going well. However, in August of 1960 the Detroit Tigers and Cleveland Indians made the only swap of Major League managers in history. Jimmy Dykes was sent to Cleveland for Joe Gordon, straight up. Ironically, both had been All-Star second basemen. In 2009, Gordon was inducted into the Hall of Fame long after his death.

Left: Jimmy Dykes.

Below: Joe Gordon.

COOPERSTOWN, NY: (L–R) Back row: Honus Wagner, Grover Cleveland Alexander, Tris Speaker, Nap Lajoie, George Sisler, Walter Johnson. (L-R) Front row: Eddie Collins, Babe Ruth, Connie Mack, and Cy Young pose for a portrait during the 1939 Hall of Fame inductions.

The Hall of Fame

There is a famous photograph taken of the initial inductees into the Baseball Hall of Fame when the museum opened in 1939 that features all but one of the stars. Ty Cobb is absent. He arrived late and missed the picture.

Besides acting as a home for Hall of Famers and gathering baseball memorabilia by the ton, the Baseball Hall of Fame in Cooperstown supervises a research library housing books and documents about the sport. Among the items on call are individual files on every single player who has appeared in a Major League game. Some of the files are very slender, containing a single item. Others bulge into file folder after file folder. All told, there are more than 16,000 such files and the collection grows every time a rookie shows up in his first game.

The first and only Canadian player elected to the Baseball Hall of Fame is pitcher Ferguson Jenkins. Jenkins threw for the Philadelphia Phillies, Boston Red Sox, Texas Rangers, and Chicago Cubs and compiled a 284–226 record in 19 seasons, winning 20 or more games in a season seven times while striking out 3,192 batters.

Least famous members of the Baseball Hall of Fame: Morgan Bulkeley, Jim O'Rourke, Tommy McCarthy, Bobby Wallace, Sam Thompson, Bill McGowan, Bid McPhee, Andy Cooper, Frank Grant, Pete Hill, Louis Santop, Ben Taylor, Sol White, and Jud Wilson.

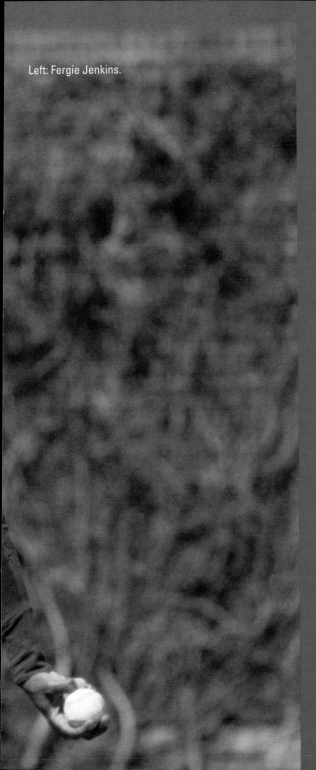

Left: Fergie Jenkins.

Voices from the Booth

Some legendary baseball broadcasters: Mel Allen, Red Barber, Bob Prince, Curt Gowdy, Vin Scully, Ernie Harwell, Jack Buck, Joe Garagiola, Bob Uecker, Jack Brickhouse, and Russ Hodges.

Once upon a time the broadcast booth was home to professionally trained announcers. But baseball began turning to former players to add color commentary shortly after World War II. Among the players-turned-broadcasters are Dizzy Dean, Lefty Gomez, Joe Garagiola, Tony Kubek, Bob Uecker, Jerry Coleman, Tim McCarver, Herb Score, Joe Nuxhall, George Kell, Jerry Remy, Ken Harrelson, Steve Stone, Ed Farmer, Rick Monday, Jim Palmer, Bert Blyleven, Ralph Kiner, Mark Grace, Ron Santo, Fernando Valenzuela, Cookie Rojas, Ron Darling, Keith Hernandez, Joe Morgan, Orel Hershiser, Jim Kaat, and Rick Sutcliffe.

Words and Pictures

Some famous photographers of baseball:

Charles Conlon,
George Brace,
George Dorrill,
George Burke,
Joseph Hall,
Don Wingfield

Artists have found baseball to be an irresistible topic over the years. Some top painters of baseball portraits and topics are:

Norman Rockwell,
Arthur Miller,
Ron Stark,
Christopher Paluso,

Some legendary baseball writers:

Ring Lardner,
Hugh Fullerton,
Red Smith,
John P. Carmichael,
Grantland Rice,
Heywood Broun,

Below: Award-winning sports writer and television personality Peter Gammons throws out the first pitch before the start of a Red Sox and Orioles game at Fenway Park.

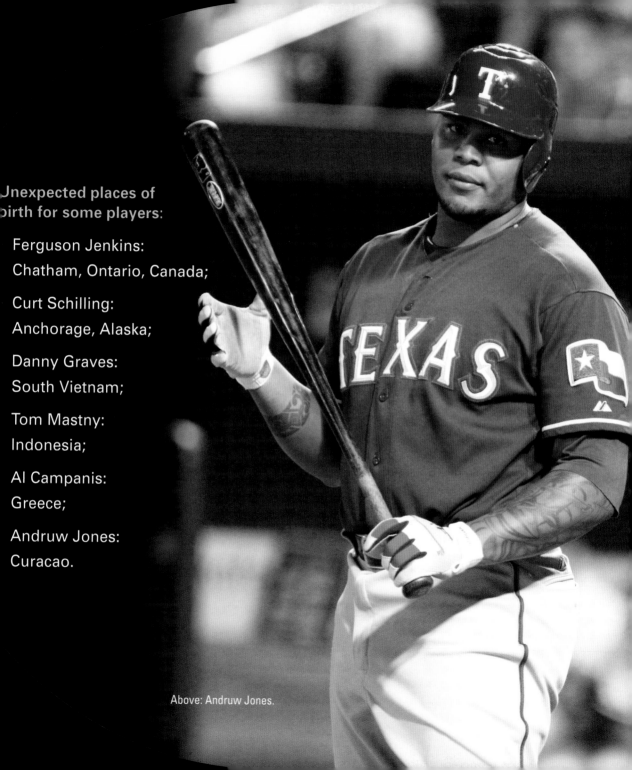

Unexpected places of birth for some players:

Ferguson Jenkins:
Chatham, Ontario, Canada;

Curt Schilling:
Anchorage, Alaska;

Danny Graves:
South Vietnam;

Tom Mastny:
Indonesia;

Al Campanis:
Greece;

Andruw Jones:
Curacao.

Above: Andruw Jones.

Global Marketing

The first player to reach the majors from the Bahamas was shortstop Andre Rodgers, who broke in with the Giants in 1957. The first player born in Czechoslovakia was outfielder Elmer Valo with the Philadelphia Athletics in 1940. The first Jamaican-born player was Chili Davis, who made his debut with the Giants in 1981.

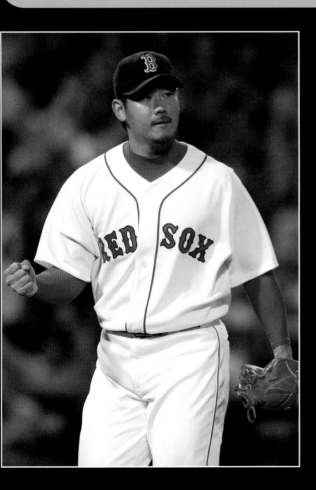

Baseball in Japan owes its roots to an American student in the field of engineering who brought the game to the country in 1872. There are two professional leagues in Japan, the Central and the Pacific Leagues. Each league has six teams. The first Japanese player to appear in the majors was pitcher Masanori Murakami for the San Francisco Giants in 1964. The greatest Japanese star of all is home-run king Sadaharu Oh, who smashed 868 career homers. In recent years several Japanese stars have made the switch to the majors, playing prominent roles in the game in the U.S. The biggest star is Ichiro Suzuki of the Seattle Mariners, who since 2001 has won the Rookie of the Year Award, an MVP award, eight Gold Gloves, two batting titles, and has been a nine-time All-Star. The most prominent pitcher to make his mark from Japan is Hideo Nomo, who came to the United States in 1995 and pitched two no-hitters. Other well-respected Japanese players in the American game include Hideki Matsui, Takashi Saito, and Daisuke Matsuzaka.

Above: Boston Red Sox pitcher Daisuke Matsuzaka.

Brotherly Love

Between the late 1880s and 1915, five brothers in the Delahanty family of Cleveland, Ohio, played Major League ball: from oldest to youngest, Ed, Tom, Jim, Frank, and Joe. Ed was the best. With a lifetime average of .346, he was elected to the Hall of Fame in 1945.

Famous Major League brother combinations:

Joe, Dom, and Vince DiMaggio;

Jerome Hanna (Dizzy) and Paul (Daffy) Dean;

Paul and Lloyd Waner;

Cal Jr. and Billy Ripken;

Frank and Joe Torre;

Hank and Tommie Aaron;

Pedro and Ramon Martinez;

Rick and Wes Ferrell;

Bret and Aaron Boone;

Felipe, Matty, and Jesus Alou;

Bengie, Jose, and Yadier Molina;

Roberto and Sandy Alomar Jr.;

Frank and Milt Bolling;

Ken, Clete, and Cloyd Boyer;

George and Ken Brett;

Tony and Billy Conigliaro;

Walker and Morton Cooper;

Joe and Phil Niekro;

Jim and Gaylord Perry;

Norm and Larry Sherry;

B. J. and Justin Upton;

and Jered and Jeff Weaver.

Left: The Torre brothers working out at the 1961 Milwaukee Braves training camp: Joe Torre (L) trying out as catcher, and brother Frank in the infield.

Family Love, Part I

Famous Major League father-son combinations:

Jose Cruz and Jose Cruz Jr.;

Tony Gwynn and Tony Gwynn Jr.;

Cecil Fielder and Prince Fielder;

Tito Francona and Terry Francona;

Ken Griffey Sr. and Ken Griffey Jr.;

Ray Boone and Bob Boone and Bob Boone and Aaron and Bret Boone;

Max Lanier and Hal Lanier;

Gus Bell and Buddy Bell and Buddy Bell and David Bell;

Felipe Alou and Moises Alou;

Ruben Amaro and Ruben Amaro Jr.;

Yogi Berra and Dale Berra;

Randy Hundley and Todd Hundley;

Bob Kennedy and Terry Kennedy;

Vern Law and Vance Law;

Sandy Alomar Sr., Sandy Alomar Jr. and Robert Alomar;

Dave LaRoche and Adam and Andy LaRoche.

Below: New York Mets third base coach Sandy Alomar Sr. with his son Sandy Alomar Jr. after a workout at the training facility in Port St. Lucie Florida in 2007.

75

Tools of the Trade

Sick of going home with bruises on his legs, catcher Roger Bresnahan (nicknamed "The Duke of Tralee" because of his Irish heritage) invented the shinguard and first used the protection in 1907 while playing for the New York Giants.

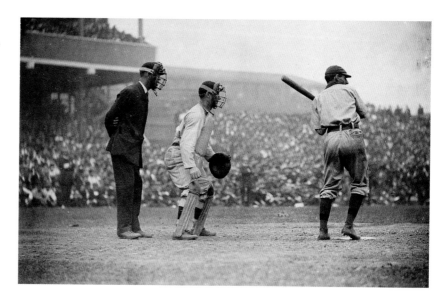

Right: Roger Bresnahan.

The Hillerich & Bradsby Company is the manufacturer of Louisville Slugger baseball bats. The firm opened in 1855 as a woodworking shop and made its first baseball bat for future Hall of Famer Pete Browning, who was playing for the local nine in 1884 when he broke his bat during a game. Founder J. F. Hillerich was not interested in making baseball bats, but his son Bud convinced him that the manufacture of the sporting equipment would be a worthwhile plan. He was right. Standing in front of company headquarters in downtown Louisville today is the "world's largest baseball bat." It is 120 feet tall, made of carbon steel, and weighs 34 tons. The actual bat model is the same design Babe Ruth used, though not even he could have swung this monster.

Right: Giant bat outside Louisville Slugger factory.

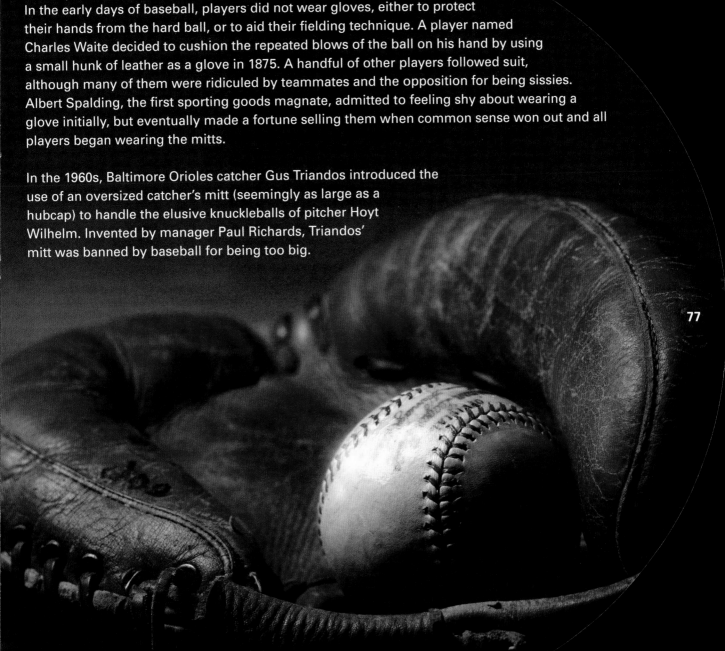

In the early days of baseball, players did not wear gloves, either to protect their hands from the hard ball, or to aid their fielding technique. A player named Charles Waite decided to cushion the repeated blows of the ball on his hand by using a small hunk of leather as a glove in 1875. A handful of other players followed suit, although many of them were ridiculed by teammates and the opposition for being sissies. Albert Spalding, the first sporting goods magnate, admitted to feeling shy about wearing a glove initially, but eventually made a fortune selling them when common sense won out and all players began wearing the mitts.

In the 1960s, Baltimore Orioles catcher Gus Triandos introduced the use of an oversized catcher's mitt (seemingly as large as a hubcap) to handle the elusive knuckleballs of pitcher Hoyt Wilhelm. Invented by manager Paul Richards, Triandos' mitt was banned by baseball for being too big.

All-Around Athletes

Right: Bob Gibson.

Far Right: Jim Thorpe.

Baseball Players Who Played Other Sports:

1) Jim Thorpe, Olympic decathlon gold medalist and pro football star;

2) Chicago Bears owner and coach George Halas played right field for the Yankees before Babe Ruth arrived;

3) New York Knicks star Dave DeBusschere pitched for the White Sox;

4) Heisman Trophy winner Bo Jackson was an All-Star outfielder;

5) All-Pro defensive back Deion Sanders was an outfielder for the Braves and other teams;

6) 1960 National League Most Valuable Player Dick Groat was an All-American basketball player for Duke;

7) Braves pitcher Gene Conley was a member of the World Champion Boston Celtics and is the only athlete to win championship rings in baseball and basketball;

8) Hall of Fame pitcher Ferguson Jenkins played for the Harlem Globetrotters;

9) Hall of Fame pitcher Bob Gibson was a basketball star for Creighton and played for the Harlem Globetrotters;

10) 19-year Major League pitcher Ron Reed also played in the NBA;

11) Michael Jordan, acclaimed by many as the best basketball player ever, played one year of AA baseball in Birmingham in the White Sox organization.

Bill Sharman, one of only three men to be enshrined in the Basketball Hall of Fame as a player and coach, was a minor-league baseball star who had a September call-up in 1951 for the Dodgers, but never got into a game. He watched from the bench as the Giants defeated Brooklyn on Bobby Thomson's home run to win the National League pennant.

Possibly the greatest rise through the ranks of any figure in baseball history belonged to Buddy LeRoux, who started his career as trainer for the Boston Celtics and Bruins, then the Red Sox, and ultimately became a key part-owner of the Red Sox.

The second George Bush to become president of the United States had been governor of Texas in his previous elected office. But his other high-profile job was as managing partner of the Texas Rangers' American League ball club.

Right: American League club presidents and the American League President, Ban Johnson, pose in 1914. Back row (L–R): Frank Navin (Detroit); Benjamin S Minor (Washington); Frank Farrell (New York). Front row (L–R): Charles Comiskey (Chicago); Ban Johnson; Joseph Lannin (Boston).

81

The All-Star Game

As the brainchild of Chicago Tribune sports editor Arch Ward, the Major League Baseball All-Star Game was supposed to be a one-time event held at Comiskey Park in conjunction with the Chicago World's Fair of 1933. Seizing upon the premise, the Negro Leagues also inaugurated its East-West All-Star Game that season, also held at Comiskey Park. When the Major League All-Star Game reached its 50th anniversary in 1983, that game, too, was played at Comiskey Park.

Appropriately, when the first All-Star Game was held in Chicago in 1933, the first player to hit a home run in the contest was Babe Ruth. Ruth cracked his wallop in the third inning.

Three outfielders have made the most appearances in baseball's annual All-Star Game. Hank Aaron, Willie Mays, and Stan Musial each played in 24 games during their careers.

Below: Pre-game ceremonies for the 79th Annual Baseball All-Star game at Yankee Stadium. in 2008

83

The Commissioners

These are the nine men who have been commissioner of baseball:

1) Judge Kenesaw Mountain Landis, 1920–1944;

2) Albert "Happy" Chandler, 1945–1951;

3) Ford Frick, 1951–1965;

4) William Eckert, 1965–1968;

5) Bowie Kuhn, 1969–1984;

6) Peter Ueberroth, 1984–1988;

7) Bart Giamatti, 1989;

8) Fay Vincent, 1989–1992;

9) Allan "Bud" Selig, 1992–present.

Diamond Laughs

Left: Portrait of former Los Angeles Dodgers players (clockwise, from top left) Rick Monday, Jerry Reuss, Jay Johnstone, and Steve Yeager. They were part of the Dodgers' Big Blue Wrecking Crew in the early 1980s.

Left: Judge Landis prepares to throw out the first baseball at the opening of the World Series between the St. Louis Cardinals and the New York Yankees. At left a distinguished British visitor, Field Marshal Viscount Allenby, who was the guest of the American Legion.

Some of the funniest men in baseball history:

Nick Altrock, Jimmy Dykes, Max Patkin, Joe Garagiola, Yogi Berra, Steve "Psycho" Lyons, Bill "Spaceman" Lee, Mark Fidrych, Ryan Dempster, Ozzie Guillen, Al Schacht, Casey Stengel, Harry Caray, Mickey Rivers, Jimmy Piersall, Dizzy Dean, Lefty Gomez, Rube Waddell, Bill Veeck, Moe Drabowsky, and Jay Johnstone.

Baseball in Wartime

In a patriotic gesture, Major League Baseball cut short the 1918 season as the United States' involvement in World War I heated up. Teams played approximately 130 games and the World Series was completed. However, the armistice was declared November 11, ending hostilities, and play resumed normally the next spring. The Boston Red Sox won the 1918 Series, their last until 2004.

Above: Sam Agnew of 1918 Red Sox.

Singing of the "Star Spangled Banner" before the start of Major League
Baseball games became a tradition as the United States was heading into World
War II in 1941. The National Hockey League had already adopted the practice of
singing "Oh, Canada," before its games.

When World War II started and the United States was mobilizing its troops, baseball
commissioner Kenesaw Mountain Landis wrote to President Franklin Delano Roosevelt asking
if it was appropriate for the sport to be played while the nation was at war. Roosevelt wrote back
saying baseball was good recreation for those at home. The response became known as "the
green light letter," and it enabled Major League Baseball to continue play.

The All-America Girls Professional Baseball League was formed during World War II to provide
additional baseball entertainment for the public at a time when many top male players were off at
war, minor league teams were jeopardized, and ballparks lay fallow. P. K. Wrigley, owner of the Cubs,
was the impetus behind creation of the league, which was established in 1943 and met its demise in
1954. Among the cities that fielded teams were Racine and Kenosha, Wisconsin, Rockford, Illinois, and
South Bend, Indiana. The story of the league was told in the popular movie, *A League of Their Own*.

Left: Shirley Jamison reaches
third base as Ann Harnett
bends down for the catch
during a 1943 team practice.
The teammates are members of
the Kenosha Comets, one of the
four original teams of the All-
American Girls Professional
Baseball League.

Pitcher Joe Nuxhall is the youngest player to appear in a Major League game. Due to a manpower shortage during World War II, Nuxhall was put into the Cincinnati Reds lineup in 1944 when he was just 15 years, 316 days old. Nuxhall's next appearance in the majors was not until 1952. He played 16 seasons, won 135 games and then embarked on a long broadcasting career.

Hall of Fame players whose careers were interrupted significantly by World War II: Bob Feller, Hank Greenberg, Joe DiMaggio, Warren Spahn, Bob Lemon, Pee Wee Reese, and Ted Williams. Williams was also called to serve during the subsequent Korean War.

Of the 500 major leaguers who served in the military during World War II (35 of them eventually members of the Hall of Fame), two died in action. They were Harry O'Neill and Elmer Gedeon. O'Neill played in just one game for the Philadelphia Athletics in 1939 and Gedeon played in just five games for the Washington Senators in 1939.

Left: Ted Williams in 1950 when he was in the U.S. Navy Reserve. He would go on to fly combat missions in Korea in 1953.

Right: Bob Feller in 1937.

89

Right: U.S. President Barack Obama throws out the ceremonial first pitch prior to Major League Baseball's All-Star game in St. Louis July 14, 2009.

On August 30, 1865, President Andrew Johnson invited a baseball team to the White House simply called National Base Ball Club, starting a trend that continues today, though usually only with championship teams. Johnson was the first to refer to baseball as The National Game. The phrase "National Pastime" to describe baseball passed into lexicon.

Benjamin Harrison was the first president to witness a Major League game in 1892.

In 1910, President William Howard Taft became the first leader of the United States to throw out the first pitch when he kicked off the season by tossing the ball to Walter Johnson at a Washington Senators game.

In 1937, FDR became the first president to throw out the first pitch at an All-Star Game. Richard Nixon did so in 1970, as did Barack Obama in 2009.

Right: President Taft tossing out the first ball in 1910.

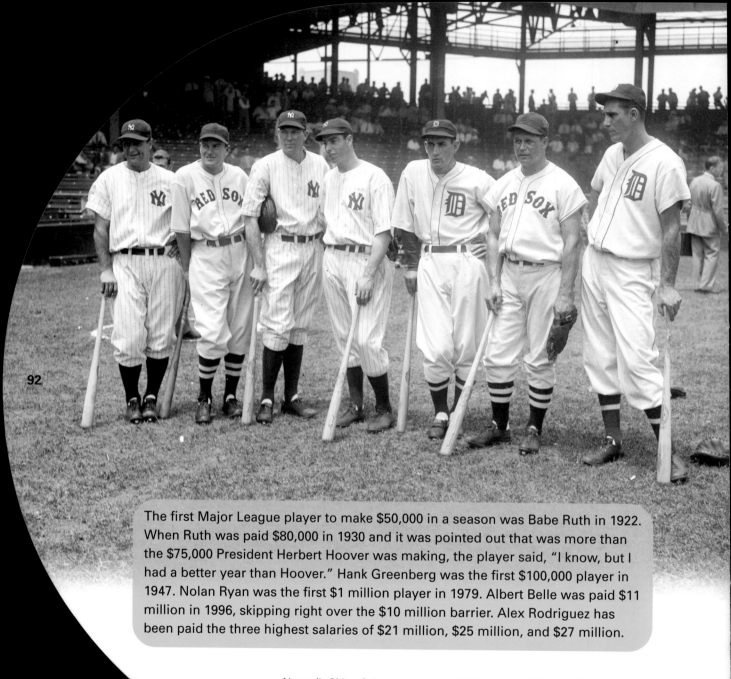

The first Major League player to make $50,000 in a season was Babe Ruth in 1922. When Ruth was paid $80,000 in 1930 and it was pointed out that was more than the $75,000 President Herbert Hoover was making, the player said, "I know, but I had a better year than Hoover." Hank Greenberg was the first $100,000 player in 1947. Nolan Ryan was the first $1 million player in 1979. Albert Belle was paid $11 million in 1996, skipping right over the $10 million barrier. Alex Rodriguez has been paid the three highest salaries of $21 million, $25 million, and $27 million.

Above: (L–R) Lou Gehrig, Joe Cronin, Bill Dickey, Joe DiMaggio, Charlie Gehringer, Jimmie Foxx, and the first $100,000 player, Hank Greenberg, in a 1937 lineup.

Right: Scramble for FDR's opening pitch for the 1937 All-Star Game.

The first night game in Major League history was played at Crosley Field in Cincinnati on May 24, 1935. The Reds hosted the Philadelphia Phillies and won the game, 2–1. Through a special hookup, President Franklin Delano Roosevelt was able to throw the switch lighting up the stadium 600 miles from the White House.

Taking One for the Team

Craig Biggio, the longtime second baseman for the Houston Astros who retired in 2007 and is a likely Hall of Famer, holds the Major League record for being hit by a pitch the most times in his career with 285. He broke the record set by outfielder Don Baylor, who had been hit 267 times when he retired in 2005. Ron Hunt, a second baseman with the Mets, previously held the record with 243 plunkings. Hunt once said, "Some people give their bodies to science, I give mine to baseball."

Left: Houston Astros batter Craig Biggio takes one on the shoulder from Florida Marlins pitcher A.J. Burnett.

The Ballparks

Early in baseball's history ballparks were primarily made of wood. The first concrete and steel ballpark was opened in 1909 in Philadelphia. Called Shibe Park, the field was later renamed Connie Mack Stadium.

The oldest ballpark in the major leagues is Fenway Park, home of the Boston Red Sox. The structure opened in 1912—the same week that the Titanic sank. For many years, frustrated fans of the Red Sox believed that was no coincidence.

Fenway Park is the oldest ballpark in the majors, but the Boston American League franchise needed a place to play before that. The Bostonians' prior home was the Huntington Avenue Grounds, from 1901 to 1911. Built on a one-time circus lot, the deep center field distance from home plate was originally a robust 530 feet. In 1908 it was expanded to a ridiculous 635 feet. No one was going to hit a home run in that direction (especially in the dead ball era) without employing a cannon.

Beloved Wrigley Field, known as "The Friendly Confines," and home of the Chicago Cubs, was built in 1914. Initially it served a Federal League team and was called Weeghman Park. When that league went out of business, the field reverted to the Cubs with the name of Cubs Park. In 1926, Wrigley became Wrigley.

Right: Wrigley Field is known for its greenery.

Far Right: Shibe Park.

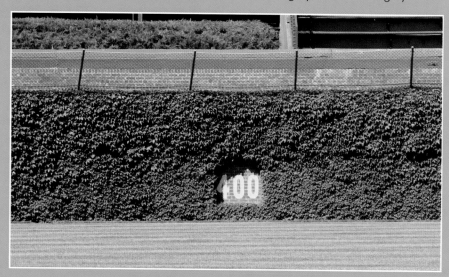

The original Yankee Stadium opened in 1923 and was known as "The House That Ruth Built" because Babe Ruth's slugging prowess created unprecedented demand for tickets. Capacity was 56,866. It cost $2.5 million to build. The new Yankee Stadium opened in 2009. Capacity is 52,325. It is estimated that final costs of construction will be $1.3 billion.

When the New York Yankees moved into the new Yankee Stadium for the start of the 2009 season, the best seats in the house were priced at $2,500. For that fee, fans received a ticket, parking, food and service from waiters, plus access to special private clubs. Coming at a time when the nation was in an economic slump, however, the 1,800 tickets per game were not especially popular.

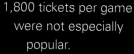

Inset: The New Yankee Stadium's Monument Park.

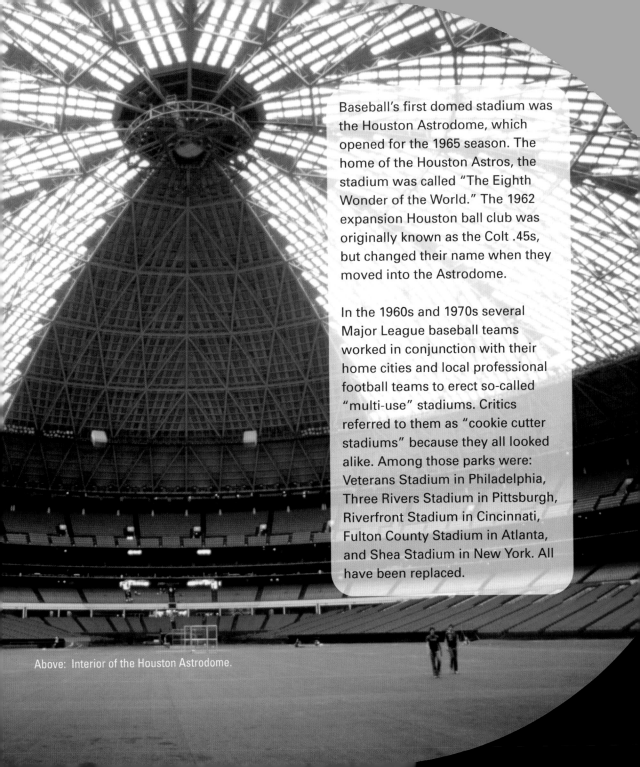

Baseball's first domed stadium was the Houston Astrodome, which opened for the 1965 season. The home of the Houston Astros, the stadium was called "The Eighth Wonder of the World." The 1962 expansion Houston ball club was originally known as the Colt .45s, but changed their name when they moved into the Astrodome.

In the 1960s and 1970s several Major League baseball teams worked in conjunction with their home cities and local professional football teams to erect so-called "multi-use" stadiums. Critics referred to them as "cookie cutter stadiums" because they all looked alike. Among those parks were: Veterans Stadium in Philadelphia, Three Rivers Stadium in Pittsburgh, Riverfront Stadium in Cincinnati, Fulton County Stadium in Atlanta, and Shea Stadium in New York. All have been replaced.

Above: Interior of the Houston Astrodome.

As a method of marketing and luring children into the ballpark to watch baseball, teams for decades have offered promotional items as giveaways. Some popular items passed out for free with the purchase of a game ticket: bats, caps, baseball cards, schedules, baseballs, key chains, stuffed animals, replicas of World Series championship rings, water bottles, pens, and lately bobble-head likenesses of players.

Famous ballparks demolished or abandoned: Ebbets Field in Brooklyn, the Polo Grounds in New York, Forbes Field in Pittsburgh, Shibe Park (aka Connie Mack Stadium) in Philadelphia, Municipal Stadium in Cleveland, Griffith Stadium in Washington, D.C., County Stadium in Milwaukee, Candlestick Park in San Francisco, Sportsman's Park in St. Louis, Briggs Stadium in Detroit, Yankee Stadium in New York, and Comiskey Park in Chicago. The new Yankee Stadium, opened in 2009, is across the street from the original Yankee Stadium. The new White Sox stadium, opened in 1991, is across the street from the original Comiskey Park. The new Chicago field was originally called New Comiskey Park, but was changed to U.S. Cellular Field in 2003.

Peculiar dimensions of ballparks no longer used by Major League teams: the original right field distance in old Yankee Stadium was 295 feet; the distance down the left field line in the Los Angeles Coliseum was 251 feet; the distance to center field in Forbes Field was 442 feet; the height of the Green Monster left field wall at Fenway Park is 37 feet, 2 inches.

Right: Forbes Field.

Quiz #4: Name that Ballpark

CAN YOU IDENTIFY THE MLB BALLPARKS FROM THESE GROUND PLANS?

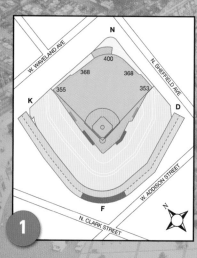

1

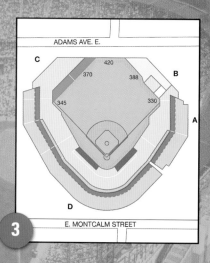

2

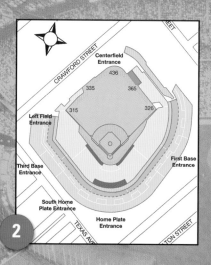

3

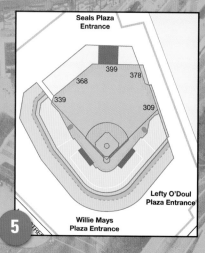

4

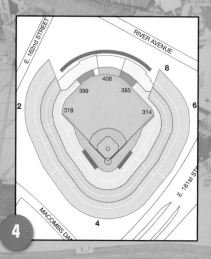

5

Answers on page 104

Simply the Best

Everyone knows that Fenway Park is the oldest of all current Major League Baseball stadiums and has remained the same since 1912 because you can't beat perfection.

The home ballpark of the Boston Red Sox, Fenway Park gets its name from its location in the Fenway district of Boston which was created late in the nineteenth century by filling in marshland or "fens." It opened on April 20, 1912, six days after the sinking of the *Titanic*, and proved rather longer lasting. It has had its bad years—but not recently: on September 8, 2008, with a game versus the Tampa Bay Rays, Fenway Park broke the all-time Major League record with its 456th consecutive sellout. Its capacity has changed little, oscillating between 35,000 in 1912 and 2008 night games' toital of 37,400.

Fenway hosted the Major League Baseball All-Star Game in 1946, 1961, and 1999, and has played host to nine World Series. It has also been the location of many other sporting and cultural events. Professional football teams the Boston Redskins and the Boston Patriots both spent several seasons playing home games at the park. Musicians such as Bruce Springsteen and Jimmy Buffett have performed at Fenway Park, and President Franklin D. Roosevelt gave his last campaign speech there in 1944.

Historically, Fenway Park has been decidedly unfriendly to left-handed pitchers, Babe Ruth being

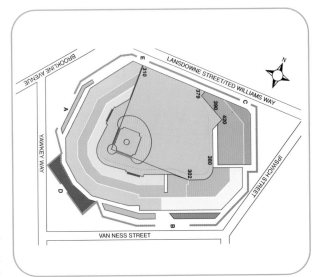

one of the few southpaw exceptions. Ruth started his career as a pitcher (mostly during the "dead-ball era"), and had a career record of 94 wins, 46 losses (.671 winning percentage). Ruth also set a World Series record by pitching 29²⁄₃ scoreless innings, a record that lasted until broken by Whitey Ford of the New York Yankees in 1961.

Ballpark Food

The hot dog has been a staple of ballpark food for more than a century. Available at all stadiums in one form or another, currently teams offer hot dogs under specialty names that relate to the ball club or the region of the country where they can be obtained. In Los Angeles, Dodger Dogs are for sale. In Boston, Fenway Franks are the item of choice. There is a Cincinnati Cheesy Coney and a Milwaukee Brat. The first purveyor of hot dogs in a stadium was the St. Louis Browns in 1893.

104

Through tradition and longstanding sales, routine ballpark food is considered to include hot dogs, peanuts, Cracker Jack, and cotton candy. In more recent years, due to changing tastes, some ballparks have added sushi, tacos, salmon, espresso, knishes, and Rocky Mountain oysters. Another staple item is beer, but it has been supplemented by wine and margaritas at various locales.

Above: Cotton candy.

Right: Opening day of the 1959 World Series finds fans lined up outside of Comiskey Park as the White Sox and Dodgers prepare to meet in baseball's annual classic. About 50,000 fans attended the game.

Answer to Quiz #4: 1. Wrigley Field: 2. Minute Maid Park: 3. Comerica Park: 4. Yankee Stadium (new): 5. AT&T Park:

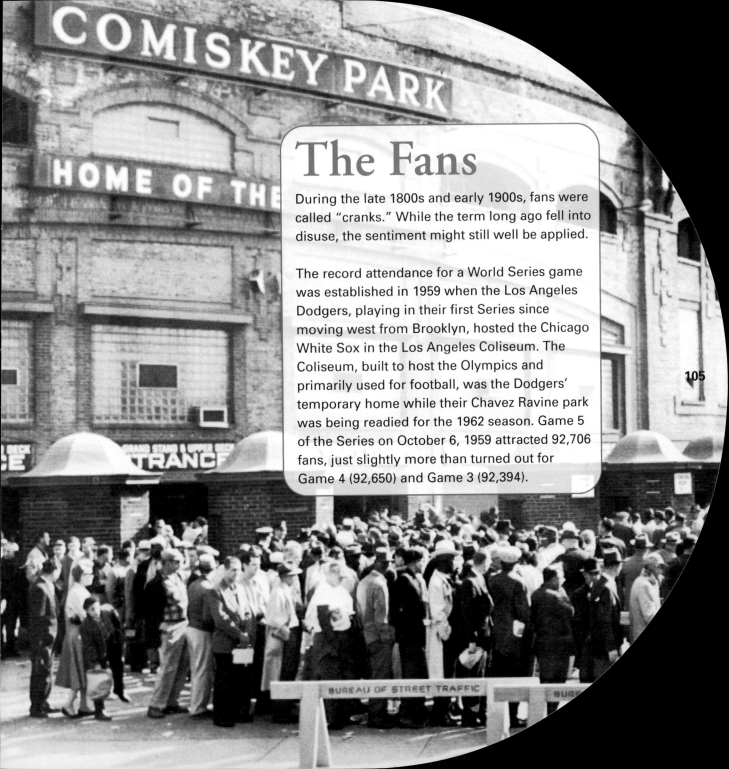

The Fans

During the late 1800s and early 1900s, fans were called "cranks." While the term long ago fell into disuse, the sentiment might still well be applied.

The record attendance for a World Series game was established in 1959 when the Los Angeles Dodgers, playing in their first Series since moving west from Brooklyn, hosted the Chicago White Sox in the Los Angeles Coliseum. The Coliseum, built to host the Olympics and primarily used for football, was the Dodgers' temporary home while their Chavez Ravine park was being readied for the 1962 season. Game 5 of the Series on October 6, 1959 attracted 92,706 fans, just slightly more than turned out for Game 4 (92,650) and Game 3 (92,394).

The record for the largest single-season attendance by a Major League team was set by the Colorado Rockies in 1993 when the club drew 4,483,350 fans. The New York Yankees (high of 4,298,655 in 2008), the Toronto Blue Jays (4,057,947 in 1993), and the New York Mets (4,042,045 in 2008) are the other teams that have attracted more than four million fans in a season. The Yankees have done so four times and the Blue Jays three times.

Between June 12, 1995 and April 4, 2001, the Cleveland Indians set a Major League record by selling out 455 games at Jacobs Field. The record did not last long. The Boston Red Sox eclipsed that mark on September 9, 2008 when the 456th straight sellout was recorded at Fenway Park. The Boston streak continued through the end of the 2008 season and the Red Sox hit their 500th straight sellout on June 17, 2009. The streak was ongoing through the 2009 season.

Morganna the Kissing Bandit was in her Major League heyday in the 1970s and 1980s. A one-time stripper who also posed for *Playboy magazine*, Morganna was known for her extraordinarily large bust-line. She used to buy front-row seats at stadiums and dash onto the field to kiss a player before being arrested and escorted out of the building. She traveled the country, purchasing seats in various ballparks, then leaping over the wall onto the field interrupting play. Her first target was Pete Rose at Riverfront Stadium in Cincinnati in 1971, and she also landed smooches on Nolan Ryan, Len Barker, Cal Ripken Jr., Johnny Bench, and Steve Garvey, among others. Morganna, who made the rounds of late-night talk-show hosts after she gained notoriety, said she kissed Rose to win a bet from a friend. She took to saying of the all-time hits leader disgraced for betting on baseball, "I tell people my career started with a bet, and Pete's ended with one."

Left: A packed crowd tries to get into the Polo Grounds, New York, for the 1911 World Series.

Below: Nolan Ryan gets ready to receive a kiss from Morganna in 1985.

Baseball Cards and Collectibles

The most valuable baseball card of all time is the T-206 Honus Wagner card from 1909–1911. Produced as part of a three-season set, the Wagner card provoked the Flying Dutchman to demand his visage be withdrawn from distribution because he was opposed to the use of the tobacco items it accompanied. That created an immediate shortage, and as time passed and the scarcity of the card was proven, it gained in value. One T-206 Wagner card has sold for $2.8 million. As part of a display (behind glass) at the Hall of Fame, the card was labeled "The Holy Grail."

Left: Honus Wagner appeared on the most valuable baseball card of all time.

Right: Collage of old baseball cards.

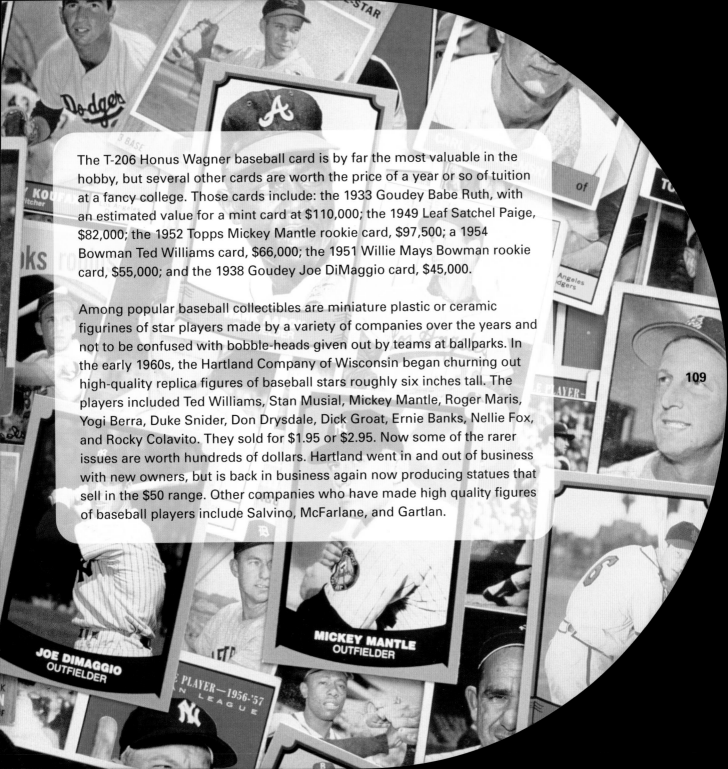

The T-206 Honus Wagner baseball card is by far the most valuable in the hobby, but several other cards are worth the price of a year or so of tuition at a fancy college. Those cards include: the 1933 Goudey Babe Ruth, with an estimated value for a mint card at $110,000; the 1949 Leaf Satchel Paige, $82,000; the 1952 Topps Mickey Mantle rookie card, $97,500; a 1954 Bowman Ted Williams card, $66,000; the 1951 Willie Mays Bowman rookie card, $55,000; and the 1938 Goudey Joe DiMaggio card, $45,000.

Among popular baseball collectibles are miniature plastic or ceramic figurines of star players made by a variety of companies over the years and not to be confused with bobble-heads given out by teams at ballparks. In the early 1960s, the Hartland Company of Wisconsin began churning out high-quality replica figures of baseball stars roughly six inches tall. The players included Ted Williams, Stan Musial, Mickey Mantle, Roger Maris, Yogi Berra, Duke Snider, Don Drysdale, Dick Groat, Ernie Banks, Nellie Fox, and Rocky Colavito. They sold for $1.95 or $2.95. Now some of the rarer issues are worth hundreds of dollars. Hartland went in and out of business with new owners, but is back in business again now producing statues that sell in the $50 range. Other companies who have made high quality figures of baseball players include Salvino, McFarlane, and Gartlan.

The Iron Men

Cal Ripken Jr., who played 21 seasons with the Baltimore Orioles, set the record for playing in the most consecutive games with 2,632. He broke Lou Gehrig's record of 2,130 straight games. Other long playing streaks in Major League history: Everett Scott, 1,307; Steve Garvey, 1,207; Miguel Tejada, 1,152; Billy Williams, 1,117; and Joe Sewell, 1,103.

Right: Cal Ripken acknowledges the applause of the New York Yankees after sitting out the game that ended his consecutive games played streak at 2,632.

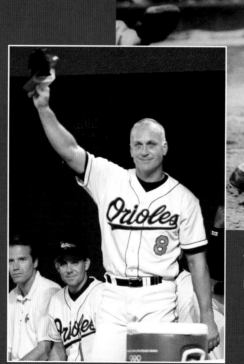

Above: Lou Gehrig.

Right: Don Mattingly.

Some of the most unheralded people who wear Major League baseball uniforms are coaches. Every team has a hitting coach, however, and some of the most respected in history are: Charlie Lau, Walt Hriniak, Terry Crowley, Hal McRae, Tommy McCraw, Gene Tenace, Gene Clines, Don Mattingly, and Wally Moses.

Some well-respected pitching coaches: Johnny Sain, Stan Williams, Mel Stottlemyre, Cal McLish, Sal Maglie, Dave Righetti, Larry Rothschild, Ray Berres, Ron Perranoski, Leo Mazzone, Ray Miller, Mel Harder, and Art Fowler.

For the Record Books

Some baseball records unlikely ever to be broken:

- Cy Young's 511 wins
- Cy Young's 318 losses
- Cy Young's 749 complete games
- Nolan Ryan's 7 no-hitters
- Joe DiMaggio hitting safely in 56 straight games
- Jack Chesbro's 41 wins in a single season
- Hack Wilson's 191 runs batted in during a single season
- Walter Johnson's 110 career shutouts

Above: Hack Wilson.

The 1930 season saw an explosion of hitting success with records established that lasted for decades (or that still endure). Hack Wilson of the Chicago Cubs drove in 191 runs, a still-standing Major League mark. Wilson also hit 56 home runs, a National League record that lasted until 1998. The Philadelphia Phillies finished last in the eight-team NL with a 52–102 record despite setting still-standing team records of most runs, hits, singles, doubles, total bases, and batting average. Philly hit .315 as a squad that year. Outfielder Chuck Klein scored 158 runs, cracked 59 doubles, drove in 170 runs, and notched a .687 slugging percentage, again all team records that still stand.

New York Yankee outfielder Joe DiMaggio recorded the longest hitting streak in baseball history when he batted safely in 56 straight games in 1941. After failing to obtain a hit in the 57th game, DiMaggio followed up by hitting in 16 consecutive games, or in 72 out of 73. Lesser known is the fact that DiMaggio had a 61-game hitting streak with the San Francisco Seals in the minors in 1933.

Left: Joe DiMaggio salutes his bat in 1941

114

In 1948, the Boston Red Sox and the Cleveland Indians tied for the American League pennant. At the end of the 154-game season each team had a record of 96–58. What followed was the first one-game playoff in Major League history to decide a participant in the World Series. Cleveland won and then took the title, the Indians' last championship.

Above: The Cleveland Indians in the locker room after beating the Red Sox in the pennant playoff, October 4, 1948, giving Cleveland its first pennant in 28 years. The happy faces belong to (L–R), Bill Veeck, president of the club, Steve Gromeck, and winning pitcher, Gene Bearden.

The New York Yankees' 40 pennants are by far the most won by any Major League team. The Yankees had three separate dynastic eras: 1921–1928 when they won six pennants in eight years; 1936–1943, when they won seven pennants in eight years; and 1947–1964 when they won 15 in 18 years. They also had mini-dynasties between 1976 and 1981 when they won four pennants in six years, and 1996–2001, when they won five pennants in six years.

Left: Roger Maris.

The longest Major League game of all time was contested on May 1, 1920 between the Boston Braves and the Brooklyn Dodgers. It lasted 26 innings and ended in a 1–1 tie because of darkness. The longest Major League game based on time played was a May 9–10 encounter between the Chicago White Sox and the Milwaukee Brewers that took 8 hours, 6 minutes to complete. Chicago won 7–6 in 25 innings. The longest professional game of all was a AAA minor-league game between the Pawtucket Red Sox and Rochester Red Wings. The game began on April 16, 1981 and its conclusion was postponed until June 23. Pawtucket won 3–2, after scoring in the bottom of the 33rd inning.

In 2001, the Seattle Mariners set an American League record, winning 116 games in the regular season, tying the 95-year-old mark set by the Chicago Cubs. The Mariners did not reach the World Series, losing in the AL playoffs.

Left: Lou Brock (left) of the St. Louis Cardinals, Carl Yastrzemski (center) of the Boston Red Sox , and Pete Rose (right) of the Philadelphia Phillies compare bats and swings at the 50th Major League Baseball All-Star Game at the Kingdome in Seattle.

Barry Bonds holds the record for most home runs in a career with 762 and most home runs in a season with 73. But he also holds the Major League record for walks in one season with 232 in 2004 and for a career with 2,558. In 2004, representative of his status as the most feared slugger in the game, Bonds was walked 120 times intentionally.

118

Near the end of the 2008 season, the Chicago White Sox obtained Ken Griffey Jr. The Sox already featured Jim Thome as designated hitter. When the two men appeared in the same batting order, it marked the first time in Major League history that teammates were members of the 500-home-run club (Thome) and the 600-home-run club (Griffey).

On April 13, 2009, Chicago White Sox teammates Jermaine Dye and Paul Konerko hit their career 300th home runs in back-to-back at-bats against the Tigers in Detroit. This was the first time in Major League history that teammates had recorded milestone hits of any denomination in consecutive plate appearances.

Only 29 years old after his first nine seasons in the majors, the St. Louis Cardinals' Albert Pujols is off to one of the best career starts in baseball history. He has hit at least 30 home runs, driven in 100, and batted at least .300 in every year he has played. That is a Major League record.

When Yankees third baseman Alex Rodriguez hit his 500th home run during the 2007 season, he was the youngest player to reach the milestone. The blow came when he was 32 years and eight days old.

119

Left: Bonds crosses the plate after hitting home run number 756.

Above: Albert Pujols.

Team Moves and Expansion

The Braves and Athletics are the only two Major League teams to represent three different cities with the same nickname. The Braves franchise got its start in Boston, moved to Milwaukee, and then to Atlanta. The Athletics were founded in Philadelphia, played in Kansas City, and now reside in Oakland.

The team representing Washington, D.C. in the major leagues has three times been called the Senators and now is called the Nationals. The first Senators team was in the American Association and the National League between 1891 and 1899. The first American League Senators team was located in the city from 1901 to 1960 and then became the Minnesota Twins. The second American League Senators joined the AL in 1961 and lasted until 1971 before becoming the Texas Rangers. The current Nationals club has been in the National League since 2005 and used to be the Montreal Expos.

The New York Mets were founded in 1962 to fill the hole in National League play left by the departure of the Brooklyn Dodgers and New York Giants to the West Coast. Their full name (almost never used) is the Metropolitans.

The 1962 Mets expansion team is considered to be the worst Major League team of all time, finishing with a record of 40–120, in 10th and last place, 60½ games behind the pennant-winning San Francisco Giants.

Above: Casey Stengel.

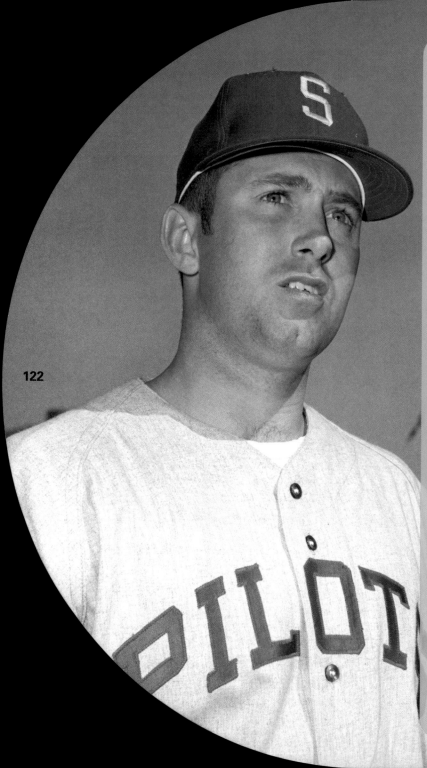

The Major League expansion team that is the fastest to win a World Series title is the Arizona Diamondbacks. Arizona began play in 1998 and won the championship in 2001, after its fourth season. The Florida Marlins began play in 1993 and won a World Series in 1997, after its fifth season. The Houston Astros began play in 1962 and have never won a World Series.

After years of play with a team in the minor league Pacific Coast League and of lobbying for a Major League franchise, Seattle was awarded an American League club called the Pilots. However, after just one year owners uprooted the team and moved it to Milwaukee to become the Brewers.

In 1969, huge changes came to the structure of Major League Baseball. Instead of play being contested solely for the reward of a National League or American League pennant, divisional play was established. Teams within leagues were broken up into separate groupings for the first time and the winners of the divisions met in a playoff format to determine the right to represent the league in the World Series. As baseball has expanded, more playoffs have been added. Presently, four teams from each league advance to postseason play, three by virtue of winning a division and a fourth by virtue of recording the next-best record among the runners-up. That team is called the "wild card."

Left: Arizona
Diamondbacks
outfielder Luis Gonzalez
(L) and New York
Yankees first baseman
Tino Martinez (R) stand
with a bat before a 2001
World Series game at
Bank One Ballpark in
Phoenix. The two
players grew up
together in Florida, have
known each other since
they were six-years-old,
and played high school
baseball together.

Far Left: Mike Marshall
pitched for the Seattle
Pilots.

The Media

KDKA in Pittsburgh broadcast the first Major League game ever on the radio on August 5, 1921. Harold Arlin was the announcer when the Pirates beat the Phillies, 8–5.

Red Barber was the announcer when the first Major League game was shown on television in 1939. W2XBS telecast a doubleheader between the Brooklyn Dodgers and the Cincinnati Reds, with each team winning one game.

Longtime famous baseball publications:

- Baseball Digest (founded 1942);

- Street and Smith Yearbook (founded in 1941, continuing as Sporting News annual since 2008);

- Who's Who In Baseball (founded 1912);

- The Sporting News (founded 1886).

Below: Red Barber.

125

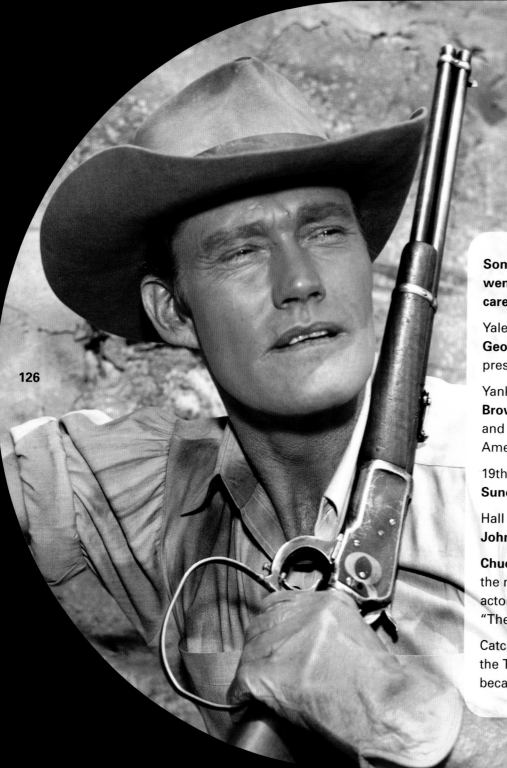

After the Cheering Stops

Some baseball players who went on to other notable careers:

Yale captain and first baseman **George H. W. Bush** became president of the United States.

Yankee third baseman **Bobby Brown** became a heart doctor and later president of the American League.

19th century outfielder **Billy Sunday** became an evangelist

Hall of Fame pitcher **Walter Johnson** ran for Congress.

Chuck Connors played briefly in the majors, then became an actor, starring in the TV series, "The Rifleman."

Catcher **Bob Uecker** starred in the TV series Mr. Belvedere and became a baseball broadcaster.

Freak Injuries

Above: Adrian Beltre.

Left: Chuck Connors in costume.

Sometimes the strangest things happen to baseball players. Some fluke injuries that put players on the bench:

- Outfielder **Sammy Sosa** sneezed and threw out his back.

- Pitcher **Fred Fitzsimmons** fell asleep in a rocking chair, dragged his hand on the ground, and crunched fingers on his pitching hand.

- Outfielder **Jose Cardenal** told management he slept awkwardly and that made his eye stick shut.

- Outfielder **Marty Cordova** fell asleep in a tanning bed and suffered burns on his face.

- Pitcher **Steve Sparks** suffered a dislocated shoulder trying to tear a phone book in half, proving he was not Superman.

- Neither is third baseman **Adrian Beltre**, who was hit in ah-hem, one of his testicles with a baseball and went on the disabled list possibly in need of surgery because he refused to wear a protective cup.

- Outfielder **Glenallen Hill** had a nightmare starring spiders, fell out of bed, and thrust his hand through some glass.

Other Levels, Other Leagues

Little League Baseball is a nonprofit organization that was founded in 1939 in Williamsport, Pennsylvania, to provide baseball team play for boys. Little League was opened to girls' participation in 1974. In 1957, a team from Monterey, Mexico became the first foreign team to win the championship.

The College World Series for NCAA Division I teams began in 1947. It has been held each June in Omaha, Nebraska, since 1950. The University of Southern California's 12 championships are the most won by a single school. Texas and Louisiana State have won six each and Arizona State has won five times.

league Mexican League into a third Major League and tried to steal established U.S. players by paying higher salaries. Certain prominent players, including Sal Maglie, Max Lanier, Mickey Owen, and Alex Carrasquel, jumped to Mexico. But the league sputtered and the players faced five-year bans from the majors by order of commissioner Happy Chandler. When the threat of the upstart league dissipated, almost all of the players were gradually reaccepted in the States.

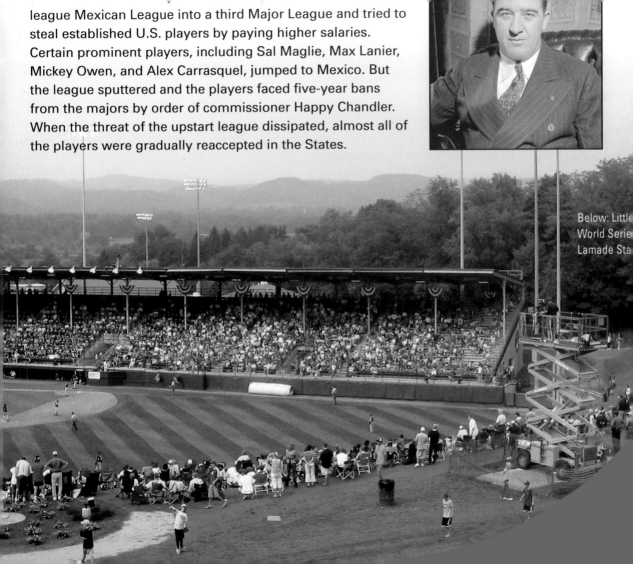

Below: Little
World Serie
Lamade Sta

Prominent players who competed summers in the Cape Cod League:
Pie Traynor, Carlton Fisk, Kevin Youkilis, Frank Thomas, Jason Varitek, Mike Lowell, Evan Longoria, Nomar Garciaparra, Lance Berkman, Jacoby Ellsbury, Tim Lincecum, Mark Teixeira, Barry Zito, Billy Wagner, Craig Biggio, Steve Stone, Thurman Munson, Bobby Valentine, Red Rolfe, Adam Kennedy, and Jeff Kent.

Above: Evan Longoria.

Considered the most unique baseball game in the world, every June 21, on the longest day of the year, the Fairbanks Goldpanners of the Alaska Baseball League host the Midnight Sun Game. A tradition in Fairbanks since 1906 in one form or another, the summer baseball team featuring collegians has conducted the event since the 1960s. The game begins at 10:30 p.m. at Growden Park and no lights are allowed during play. Spectators travel from all over the nation to see this unusual game.

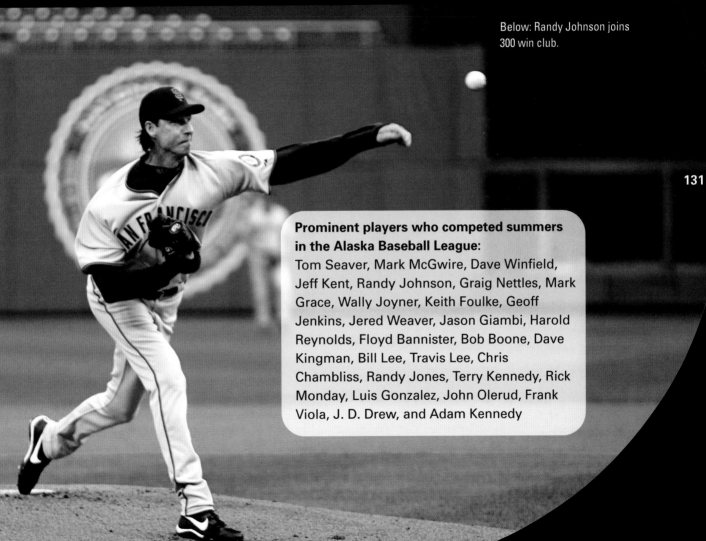

Below: Randy Johnson joins 300 win club.

Prominent players who competed summers in the Alaska Baseball League:
Tom Seaver, Mark McGwire, Dave Winfield, Jeff Kent, Randy Johnson, Graig Nettles, Mark Grace, Wally Joyner, Keith Foulke, Geoff Jenkins, Jered Weaver, Jason Giambi, Harold Reynolds, Floyd Bannister, Bob Boone, Dave Kingman, Bill Lee, Travis Lee, Chris Chambliss, Randy Jones, Terry Kennedy, Rick Monday, Luis Gonzalez, John Olerud, Frank Viola, J. D. Drew, and Adam Kennedy

Below: "The Gashouse Gang" in 1934. L–R: Jerome "Dizzy" Dean, pitcher; Leo Durocher, short stop; Frank Orsatti, center fielder; Bill Delancey, catcher; Rip Collins, first baseman; Joe Medwick, left fielder; Frank Frisch, manager and second baseman; Jack Rothrock, right fielder, and Pepper Martin, third baseman.

Team Trademarks and Catchphrases

The St. Louis Cardinals of the 1930s were known as "The Gashouse Gang" for their fun-loving ways. During an era when Major League baseball players rarely displayed facial hair, the Oakland Athletics of the early 1970s competed to grow the longest, thickest, and floweriest mustaches. They faced the Cincinnati Reds in the 1972 World Series, whose players were not allowed to grow facial hair and a wag dubbed the confrontation "the hairs versus the squares."

The 1967 Boston Red Sox were known as "The Impossible Dream" team because the team advanced from ninth place to first in one season. The Boston National League team of 1914 was known as "The Miracle Braves" because the team had finished 31½ games out of first in 1913, and even on July 15, 1914, they trailed the first-place Giants by 11½ games. The Braves then rallied to win the pennant and swept the Philadelphia A's four straight to win the World Series. "The Amazin' Mets" of 1969 had finished no higher than ninth in the National League during their first seven years of play, but came from behind to pass the Chicago Cubs to win their division, advanced to the World Series, and handled the heavily favored Baltimore Orioles.

Left: Oakland pitcher Rollie Fingers and his fine mustache.

Right: Willie Stargell, MVP of the 1979 Pittsburgh Pirates family.

Below: Frank "Tug" McGraw.

Baseball phrases that had their moment:

1) "Spahn and Sain and pray for rain," was the motto of the late 1940s Boston Braves, a team that could count on Warren Spahn and Johnny Sain as their top pitchers, but couldn't find two other reliable ones for the starting rotation.

2) "We Are Family," the theme of the 1979 World Series champion Pittsburgh Pirates, who adopted the song by that name sung by Sister Sledge;

3) "Ya Gotta Believe," was relief pitcher Tug McGraw's battle cry for the New York Mets when they rallied to win the National League pennant in 1973;

4) "Don't Stop Believin'," was the song by Journey that the 2005 World Series champion Chicago White Sox clung to as their theme;

5) "Build It and They Will Come," is the wrap-up phrase in the movie Field of Dreams about America's love affair with baseball;

6) "Don't look back, something might be gaining on you," Satchel Paige;

7) "Say-Hey," Willie Mays.

Below: Spahn and Sain.

135

You Win Some, You Lose Some

Although the 1962 New York Mets are considered the worst team of the modern era, the 1899 Cleveland Spiders might have offered a challenge given their atrocious season. In the season before the start of the 20th century, the Spiders finished 20–134 in National League play.

BEATTIN, P., Clevelands
OLD JUDGE
CIGARETTE FACTORY.
COODWIN & CO., New York.

TEBEAU, 3d B., Clevelands
OLD JUDGE
CIGARETTE FACTORY.
COODWIN & CO., New York.

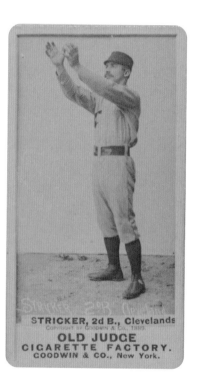

STRICKER, 2d B., Clevelands
OLD JUDGE
CIGARETTE FACTORY.
COODWIN & CO., New York.

Above: Three of the Cleveland Spiders, L–R:
P. Beattin, Patsy Tebeau, and Cub Stricker.

Spring Training

For decades Major League teams have traveled south for warm weather as they prepared for the regular season with a ritual known as spring training. The Florida-based teams are known as the Grapefruit League and the Arizona-based teams are known as the Cactus League. Although those two states represent the headquarters for spring training for all current teams, many teams have set up shop in other places over the years. For years the Chicago Cubs were famous for working out on Catalina Island in California while the island was owned by Cubs operator P. K. Wrigley. Teams have trained in Hot Springs, Arkansas, New Orleans, Havana, Cuba, Palm Springs, California, and French Lick, Indiana.

The Philadelphia Phillies, who began play in 1883, became the first franchise to lose 10,000 games in July of 2007. Phillies World Series championships came in 1915, 1980, and 2008.

Above: 1980 World Series MVP, Mike Schmidt is hoisted into the air as the Phillies celebrate victory.

Left: Cubs versus White Sox in spring training

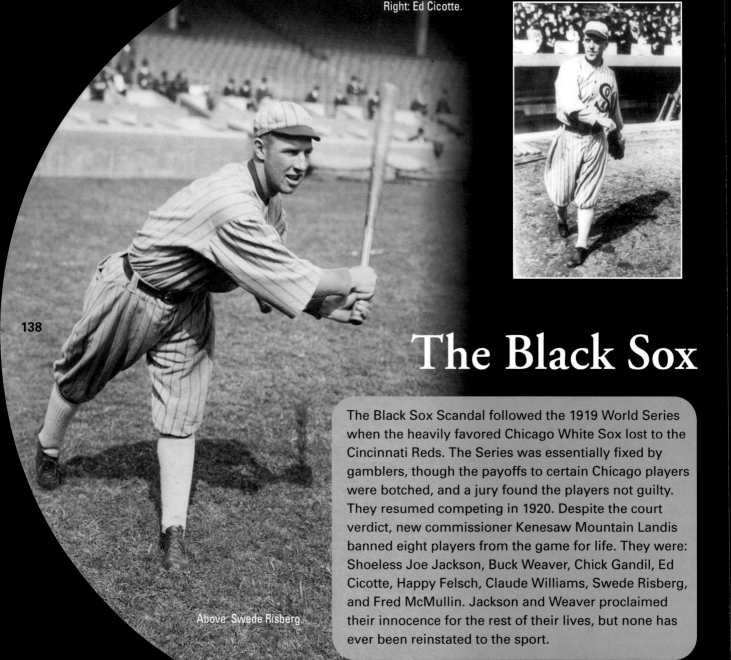

138

The Black Sox

The Black Sox Scandal followed the 1919 World Series when the heavily favored Chicago White Sox lost to the Cincinnati Reds. The Series was essentially fixed by gamblers, though the payoffs to certain Chicago players were botched, and a jury found the players not guilty. They resumed competing in 1920. Despite the court verdict, new commissioner Kenesaw Mountain Landis banned eight players from the game for life. They were: Shoeless Joe Jackson, Buck Weaver, Chick Gandil, Ed Cicotte, Happy Felsch, Claude Williams, Swede Risberg, and Fred McMullin. Jackson and Weaver proclaimed their innocence for the rest of their lives, but none has ever been reinstated to the sport.

Above: Swede Risberg.

Right: Buck Weaver.

Inset: Shoeless Joe Jackson.

The loudest campaigns in favor of reinstating banned members of the Black Sox from 1919—the group of eight players implicated in fixing the World Series—feature Shoeless Joe Jackson and Buck Weaver. Jackson was said to be illiterate and easily led. He said he gave his all in the Series. There was no evidence that Weaver did not play 100 percent, but he was punished for failing to report the scam. Like Jackson, pitcher Ed Cicotte (who collected $10,000 and was undoubtedly an active fixer) probably tossed away Hall of Fame recognition. Little remembered today for anything but the fix, Cicotte won 209 games and lost 148 in a 14-year career. He was nicknamed "Knuckles" because he was the first practitioner of the knuckleball. Also, his lifetime earned run average of 2.38 is the best ever in the modern era.

Ted Lyons finished 260–230 in a 21-year pitching career for the Chicago White Sox. For much of his career the team performed poorly consistently, after the Black Sox Scandal of 1919 resulted in stripping much of the key talent from the club. Lyons pitched until he was 46 years old. At the end of his career he took turns in the starting rotation just once a week—throwing only on Sundays.

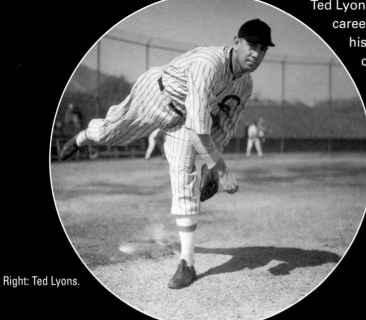

Right: Ted Lyons.

It is commonly known that the eight Chicago White Sox players implicated in the Black Sox Scandal of 1919 and all-time hits leader Pete Rose have been banned for life from Major League Baseball. However, there are numerous others on the list. There have been other suspensions, but in recent decades all except Rose have earned reinstatement. Among those from the early days of baseball still excluded long after their deaths are: Horace Fogel, in 1912, owner of the Phillies, for charging that umpires unfairly made calls against his team; Bennie Kauff of the Giants, in 1920, for selling stolen cars, despite being acquitted in court; Hal Chase, in 1921 informally banned for gambling and fixing games; Heinie Zimmerman, in 1921, for encouraging teammates to fix games; William B. Cox, in 1943, owner of the Phillies, for betting on games.

ZIMMERMANN, CHICAGO NAT'L

Above: Heine Zimmerman.

A Nasty Habit

The spitter—moistening the ball on the mound with saliva—was outlawed by Major League Baseball in 1919, but pitchers already known to be using it were grandfathered in and allowed to keep throwing it. Burleigh Grimes, who retired in 1934, was the last legal spitball thrower. However, many other pitchers have been accused of throwing a spitter or otherwise doctoring the ball with a moist substance like Vaseline. The most prominent among these in later decades are Preacher Roe of the Dodgers, Hall of Famer Gaylord Perry, and Braves star Lew Burdette. They joked that making hitters believe they threw the spitter was as valuable as actually throwing a spitball. Both Roe and Perry wrote autobiographies whose titles contained the word "spitter" or "spitball."

Substances baseball players have been known to chew (and frequently spit):

1. sunflower seeds;

2. tobacco;

3. bubble gum.

Juicing

Baseball in the 2000s has been staggered by revelations that many of its biggest stars of the 1980s, 1990s, and 2000s took performance-enhancing drugs. Through an intended-to-be anonymous survey in 2003, players testifying before Congress in committee hearings, and court cases, a number of superstars have either been implicated, confessed, faced perjury charges, or have come under serious enough suspicion to undermine their reputations. Among those who have been tainted either specifically or through public suspicion are: Barry Bonds, Roger Clemens, Alex Rodriguez, Manny Ramirez, Jason Giambi, Andy Pettitte, Mark McGwire, Sammy Sosa, Rafael Palmeiro, and David Ortiz. Most of those players never flunked a drug test and those that did so may have only failed one before baseball banned certain performance-enhancing substitutes. It remains unclear how many of the biggest stars will be excluded from election to the Hall of Fame because of the suspicion surrounding their names, or if any will.

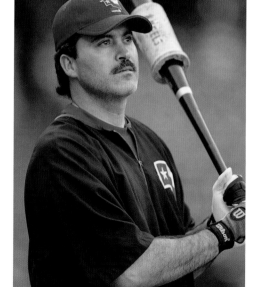

Top right: Mark McGwire hits his 500th career home run.

Right: Rafael Palmeiro.

143

Top 10 Home Run Hitters of All Time

1. Barry Bonds, 762
2. Hank Aaron, 755
3. Babe Ruth, 714
4. Willie Mays, 660
5. Ken Griffey, 627 (still active)
6. Sammy Sosa, 609
7. Frank Robinson, 586
8. Mark McGwire, 583
9. Alex Rodriguez, 579 (still active)
10. Harmon Killebrew, 573

44

Left: The controversial Barry Bonds.

Above: The incomparable Babe seen with "Black Jack"
Pershing in 1924. A great patriot, Ruth registered for the
draft in both World War I and World War II

All-Time RBI Sluggers

1. Hank Aaron, 2,297
2. Babe Ruth, 2,213
3. Barry Bonds, 1,996
4. Lou Gehrig, 1,995
5. Stan Musial, 1,951
6. Ty Cobb, 1,937
7. Jimmie Foxx, 1,922
8. Eddie Murray, 1,917
9. Willie Mays, 1,903
10. Cap Anson, 1,879

Above: Stan Musial.

Right: Jimmy Foxx.

148

Above: Lefty O'Doul.

Top 10 Career Batting Averages

1. Ty Cobb, .366

2. Rogers Hornsby, .358

3. Joe Jackson, .356

4. Lefty O'Doul, .349

5. Ed Delahanty, .346

6. Tris Speaker, .345

7. (tie) Ted Williams, .344

   Billy Hamilton, .344

9. (tie) Dan Brouthers, .342

   Babe Ruth, .342

   Dave Orr, .342

   Harry Heilman, .342

   Pete Browning, .342

Left: Tris Speaker.

Saving the Flag

Rick Monday spent 18 years as a Major League outfielder and is a longtime broadcaster for the Los Angeles Dodgers. He is most famous, however, for an occurrence on the field while competing for the Chicago Cubs. On April 25, 1976, during a road trip to Los Angeles, Monday foiled an attempt by two protesters to set the American flag on fire during a game in the outfield at Chavez Ravine. Monday swooped down and grabbed the flag away from the men, who were arrested. Monday keeps the flag in a safe deposit box most of the time, only bringing it out for select patriotic occasions. Fans were slow to realize what happened, but when Monday next came to the plate the Los Angeles fans gave him a standing ovation and the scoreboard showed a thank-you message.

Trading the Bambino

The biggest deal in Major League history: Babe Ruth was traded to the Boston Red Sox for $125,000 cash, three $25,000 notes due annually, and a $300,000 loan to Boston owner Harry Frazee. Frazee was said to have used the money to promote the Broadway play *No-No Nanette*.

Quiz #5:
Who was the first batter to come to the plate as a designated hitter? See page 152 for the answer.

Left: Harry Frazee—the man who traded the Babe.

Far Left: Rick Monday grabs the flag as two protesters try to burn it.

In 1973, the American League introduced a new weapon to the game—the designated hitter. The rule allowed teams to replace pitchers in the lineup when it was their turn to bat with a kind of permanent pinch hitter. The National League chose not to adopt the change and the leagues have played with different rules for more than 35 years. The first player to bat as a designated hitter was Ron Blomberg, then with the Yankees. Blomberg later wrote a book entitled *Designated Hebrew*.

Other great designated hitters have included Dave Parker, Hal McRae, Greg Luzinski, Paul Molitor, Don Baylor, Frank Thomas, David Ortiz, and Edgar Martinez (for whom the yearly award for best DH is named).

Answer to Quiz #5: Ron Blomberg

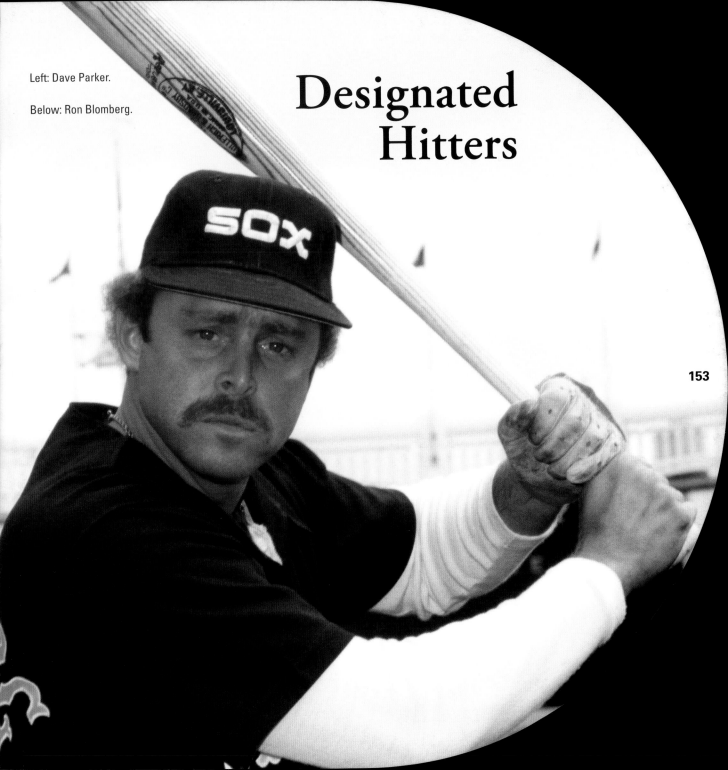

Left: Dave Parker.

Below: Ron Blomberg.

Designated Hitters

153

Mascots

Baseball's first mascot was the New York Mets' Mr. Met, introduced in 1964. The San Diego Chicken, an independent operator, became a phenomenon when he began performing shticks for the San Diego Padres in 1977. The Famous Chicken, as the mascot is also called, was still performing at baseball parks and other facilities around the nation in 2009. Besides the Chicken, the most visible, popular, and enduring mascot is the Phillie Phanatic, which made its debut in 1978 for the Philadelphia Phillies. A replica of the Phanatic is on view at the Baseball Hall of Fame and the Phanatic, Mr. Met, and Slider, the Cleveland Indians mascot, have been inducted into the relatively new (2005) Mascot Hall of Fame. There are only four Major League teams—the Yankees, Cubs, and both Los Angeles teams—that do not have a mascot. Youppi, a well-known mascot for the Montreal Expos, became defunct when the Expos moved to Washington to become the Nationals.

Inset: Phillie Phanatic, the official mascot of the Philadelphia Phillies Major League Baseball team.

Far right: New York Mets mascot "Mr. Met" entertains the fans at Shea Stadium in New York, June 4, 2005.

Fertile Ground

Baseball stars who were born in Mobile, Alabama:

1) Hank Aaron;

2) Satchel Paige;

3) Billy Williams;

4) Willie McCovey;

5) Tommie Agee;

6) Frank Bolling;

7) Amos Otis;

8) Jake Peavy;

9) Ozzie Smith.

Family Love, Part II

Pitcher Dwight Gooden is outfielder Gary Sheffield's uncle, despite being only four years older.

Red Sox outfielder J. D. Drew, Diamondbacks shortstop Stephen Drew, and former Major League pitcher Tim Drew are brothers.

Left: Donora, Pennsylvania has produced Stan Musial Ken Griffey Sr., and Ken Griffey Jr.

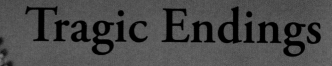

Tragic Endings

Hall of Fame outfielder Roberto Clemente played his entire 18-year Major League career with the Pittsburgh Pirates before dying tragically in a plane crash on December 31, 1972. However, Clemente was originally the property of the Dodgers, who tried to quietly stash him on a minor-league team. Branch Rickey, the same general manager who signed Jackie Robinson to break the color barrier, stole Clemente for his new team in a special draft.

Above: Roberto Clemente.

Index

159